IMAGES
of America

ANTIOCH

THE AUTHORS. Pictured, from left to right, are (first row) Phyllis Trembath Hiebert and Elizabeth A. Rimbault; (second row) Carole Ann Davis and Charles A. Bohakel. The Antioch Historical Society wishes to thank these historians for authoring this book in an unprecedented collaboration of local historians, all well known locally for their work with the Antioch Historical Society.

ON THE COVER: Pictured is the Santa Fe Depot in Antioch, *c.* 1900.

IMAGES
of America

ANTIOCH

Antioch Historical Society

Charles Bohakel, Phyllis Hiebert,
Elizabeth Rimbault, and Carole Ann Davis

ARCADIA
PUBLISHING

Published by Arcadia Publishing
Charleston, South Carolina

Library of Congress Catalog Card Number: 2005929102

For all general information contact Arcadia Publishing at:
Telephone 843-853-2070
Fax 843-853-0044
E-mail sales@arcadiapublishing.com
For customer service and orders:
Toll-Free 1-888-313-2665

Visit us on the Internet at www.arcadiapublishing.com

LANGE'S METALMARK BUTTERFLY. This lovely butterfly, with its distinctive spotted pattern, graces
the shores of the Antioch San Dunes, a former swimming area that is now a refuge administered
by the Don Edwards San Francisco Bay National Wildlife Refuge Complex. Estimated population
in recent years ranges from a few hundred to over a thousand.

CONTENTS

ACKNOWLEDGMENTS

The authors wish to thank the following for providing personal photographs and information for this book:

Antioch Historical Society; Joanne Viera Bilbo; Charles A. Bohakel; Brentwood Press, Karen Rarey; Blanche Cassin Estate; City of Antioch, Bill Gegg, and Mark Moczulski; Contra Costa History Center; Katy Cook; *Contra Costa Times*, Jose Carlos Fajardo, photographer; Carole Ann and Stan Davis; Bruna Del Chiaro; Delta Memorial Foundation; Bill Frederickson; GFWC Woman's Club of Antioch; Gordon Gravelle; Barbara Herendeen; Phyllis Trembath Hiebert; Bruce Hiebert; Earl Hohlmayer; Laura Enea Jacques; Larry S. Kramm; Joe McFarlan; Sally Roberts Massey; the Minaker family; Muriel Osborne; Millie Biglow Peterson; Thelma Biglow Giovannoni; the Rademacher family; Elizabeth Rimbault; Renny Russell; Larry Weinert; Ada Wristen; Jane Heidorn Marchione; Carol Heidorn Hughes; the journal of John Trembath; and the diary of William Wiggin Smith.

INTRODUCTION

In writing this new pictorial history of Antioch, earlier readings were dusted off, and several old, nagging questions about the beginnings of Antioch were finally answered. The end result is an awakening of knowledge about our founding fathers, William Wiggin Smith and his twin, Joseph Horton Smith; and a new awareness of the harsh environment they had to endure, both natural and man-made, to give sustaining life to this community. Of note is the fact that only W. W. Smith and Joseph H. Smith are credited with founding the town, but their wives, whose names are rarely mentioned, were at their sides every inch of the way. To give the reader a deeper understanding of our founders, we should give background of the period prior to their coming to California.

While W. W. Smith apprenticed in carpentry and architecture, twin brother Joseph H. Smith apprenticed in tailoring and attended seminary college. Both brothers were ordained as ministers. After William lost his first wife and one son of a set of twins at their birth, the surviving infant was adopted by William's brother Joseph and his wife, Sarah Lamper Smith. William later married Jane Crocker Crosswell.

Struck by gold fever, the two Smith families sailed for California on January 11, 1849. During a layover in St. Catherine, Brazil, Joseph Horton Smith contracted malaria.

Within a week of arriving in San Francisco on July 6, 1849, the families were living and working in the new settlement of New York of the Pacific (Pittsburg). While the brothers built homes and businesses, their wives and children baked bread and cakes, provided meals for lodgers, and ran a temperance dining hall. On July 19, 1849, the brothers, who had each been offered 10 acres near Marsh Landing by Dr. John Marsh on a visit to his Rancho Los Meganos, walked about 10 miles west of Marsh Landing on their return and settled two adjacent quarter sections. One is where the town of Antioch was settled and the other, including "the Point," was where William Wiggin Smith later made his home.

In August, 1849, Joseph and William divided their worldly goods. Joseph, Sarah, and their adopted son Joseph Lamper, sailed for Stockton. There he worked in the fields during the week and preached on Sundays. When he became ill, he asked William to take over his preaching engagements. William and his family left for Stockton, where he also helped to build a church. By fall, Joseph's illness was worse. He moved to New York of the Pacific, where he died in February 1850. Joseph's widow returned to running the temperance dining hall and inn, even after it was moved to Antioch.

W. W. Smith traveled to San Francisco in September 1850 to entice Capt. George W. Kimball and his newly arrived passengers from Maine to travel up the river to Antioch, with the promise of free lots and assistance in the building of homes. W. W. Smith and his family moved in and out of Antioch, traveling all over the county and northern California, building churches and schoolhouses. He was in town when a community picnic was held that gave Smith's Landing the name of Antioch.

In 1850, the U.S. government declared it would recognize legal Mexican land grants only. Land disputes became the order of the day. Both John Marsh and Lester L. Robinson, rancho owners, laid claim to land settled by Smith and settlers, who directed their anger at Smith. Court cases dragged on for 18 years, during which time Smith traveled throughout the state, building and preaching. His wife and family followed wherever he went, as indicated on the birth and death records of their five children. Ultimately he received clear title and his own U.S. land patent for Smith's Point. Not until the mid-1870s did Smith finally settle down to permanently reside at the Point until his death, three weeks after the death of his wife, Jane, in October 1899.

Actually the true founders of the town were not the Smith brothers but William Wiggin Smith and his wife, Jane Crocker Crosswell Smith, with Capt. George W. Kimball. Together they laid out the town, with Smith doing the surveying. The writing of this book has inspired a newfound need to further research William Wiggin Smith as our founding father and Jane Crocker Crosswell Smith as our founding mother.

—Compiled by Elizabeth Rimbault

One

IN THE BEGINNING

The hills, valleys, and plains of Antioch and the nearby area once provided homes for our earliest inhabitants. Anthropologists have classified the Indians of the Antioch area as Bay Miwok people. Miwok is not one language, but a family of seven genetically related languages. Antioch was also once occupied by Julpun and Ompin Indians.

Other Indians known to have come to the area, as brides from the annual great Ohlone gathering, included Ohlones (Costanoan), Patwins, Coast Miwoks, Plains Miwoks, and Yokuts.

On November 5, 1994, the City of Antioch dedicated the Native American Trails, located in the Antioch Community Park on James Donlon Boulevard. The trails include Bay Miwok Marsh Trail, Plains Miwok Trail, Miwok Trail, Yokuts Bridge, Yokuts Trail, Ohlone Creek Trail, and Patwin Access Road Trail. This was the first local dedication to the memory of the Indians.

In the 1770s, the Spanish conducted a series of land expeditions into the county to locate potential new mission sites. These contingents consisted of a commander, a padre, a few soldiers, and native guides. The earliest land exploration of the Antioch area was conducted in March 1772 by Don Pedro Fages, acting governor of Alta (Upper) California, and Padre Juan Crespi.

The next major expedition into the area was led by Capt. Juan Bautista de Anza and Padre Pedro Font in April 1776. They traveled along Suisun Bay to the fringes of the Delta. De Anza camped in the vicinity of the present-day John Nejedly Bridge (Antioch Bridge) before returning to Monterey. In October 1811, several boats undertook a 15-day trip under the command of Sgt. Jose Antonio Sanchez and Padre Ramon Abella to survey the shoreline of Contra Costa County and the Delta area.

William Wiggin Smith is credited by historians as being the founder of Antioch. The twin Smith brothers, W. W. and Joseph Horton Smith, were born in New Hampshire on August 11, 1811. In addition to trades as carpenter and tailor, both men were itinerant ministers. Following the call of gold, both brothers and their families sailed to California on the brig *Forest* and landed in San Francisco Bay on July 6, 1849. Dr. William Parker and Col. Jonathan D. Stevenson, developers of the new settlement of New York of the Pacific (Pittsburg), hired the brothers to build homes and businesses. Another earlier settler and owner of the Mexican land grant Rancho Los Meganos, Dr. John Marsh, invited the brothers to visit his ranch east of Brentwood. Marsh offered the brothers a portion of his land for $500 if they would create a new settlement. On December 24, 1849, the brothers accepted the offer and settled an area just east of downtown Antioch near Harkinson's Point (Rodgers' Point). The Smiths never paid Marsh for his land. Years later, it was discovered that Marsh only disputed the land at Smith's Point because he knew the brothers had crossed the boundary into Los Medanos Rancho.

On February 5, 1850, Joseph H. Smith died of malaria. W. W. Smith then moved to higher ground to the west overlooking the river, an area that became First Street. Smith's Point and

Smith's Landing were early names for the future community of Antioch. Later surveys of the ranchos of California would establish the border between Los Meganos Rancho and Los Medanos Rancho as being in the neighborhood of Harkinson's Point and the old Antioch Distillery wharf into the San Joaquin River.

—Compiled by Charles Bohakel and Elizabeth Rimbault

GRIZZLY IN THE TULES. The local Bay Miwok Indians used balsas made of bundles of tules that were rolled and tied together. The balsas were about 10 feet long and pointed at both ends. Double-ended paddles and long poles helped the natives to navigate local waterways. This sculpture was created by Charlotte Downs-Siska.

FISHING ALONG THE SAN JOAQUIN RIVER. The river provided local Indians with an abundance of fish. Several tribe members would work together to pull their catch to the shore with nets made of plant fibers. While the men fished, women and children gathered roots, earthworms, small animals, and insects to add to their diet. Grasshoppers were especially prized.

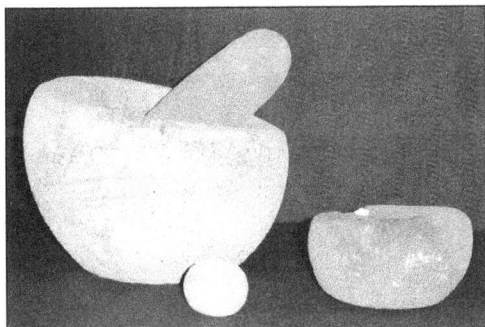

STONE MORTARS AND PESTLES. After being hulled, acorns were taken to a bedrock mortar and ground into coarse flour using a stone pestle. To remove the bitter natural tannin substances in the acorns, the flour was "leached" by making a depression in the sand at the edge of a stream, lining it with leaves and placing the flour on top of the leaves. Water was poured over the acorn flour and allowed to drain into the sand, taking the tannins with it. When the flour was dry, it was placed into a basket for cooking. This larger mortar and pestle was discovered off Wilbur Avenue near Rodgers' (Harkinson's/ Smith's) Point, lending credibility to Smith's Point being an Indian burial ground.

STORING ACORNS FOR FUTURE MEALS. Collected acorns were spread in the sun to dry, then stored in a granary made of branches tied loosely together. The structure was often six to seven feet tall and stood on legs that were two feet above ground. The bottom was lined with grass and was able to hold between 10 and 30 bushels of acorns.

THE LESSON. Charlotte Downs-Siska created this sculpture.

FAGES-CRESPI EXPEDITION, MARCH 1772. Don Pedro Fages and Padre Juan Crespi led the first land expedition into Contra Costa County. From the top of Willow Pass, the two explorers became the first Europeans to view the great expanse of the Sacramento–San Joaquin Delta. Their party, including 12 soldiers, a muleteer and an Indian guide, camped between Antioch and Pittsburg before returning to the Presidio of Monterey.

12

JOHN MARSH. The first permanent American settler in Contra Costa County, Marsh purchased Rancho Los Meganos, located in the eastern portion of the county, for $500 in 1837. He took possession of the rancho in April 1838.

JOHN MARSH STONE HOUSE. This historical house, located south of Brentwood, has been designated on the State and National Register of Historic Places.

WILLIAM WIGGIN SMITH. Pictured both as a young man and later in life, W. W. Smith was the true founder of Antioch, who initially settled on Front (First) Street, built a farm, and later bought the Point from his brother's widow. W. W. Smith and his wife, Jane, lived out their lives on the Point until their deaths, three weeks apart, in October 1899.

TOWN-NAMING PICNIC. On July 4, 1851, W. W. Smith held a picnic for the town residents on the bluff overlooking the river near his home. Between 30 and 40 men, women, and children attended and discussed the naming of the community. Smith finally suggested the biblical name of Antioch, a town in Syria where the Christians were first named. Antioch was the name chosen and dedicated to the memory of Rev. Joseph Horton Smith, who had died the previous year. This mural was painted by Charlotte Downs-Siska.

WILLIAM W. SMITH'S "NEW YORK HOUSE." Once located at the foot of Kimball (F) Street on Front (First) Street, this two-story frame structure was built in Pittsburg by the Smiths. It was later floated up the river on a barge and installed on this bluff overlooking the San Joaquin River. Following the death of Joseph H. Smith, his widow, Sarah, earned a living by operating a temperance dining hall, bakery, and inn.

HOME OF CAPTAIN KIMBALL. This home was built in the fall of 1850 on the southeast corner of Brown and Kimball (Third and F) Streets. On September 16, 1850, after sailing from New England to San Francisco Bay and being encouraged by W. W. Smith to sail upriver, the captain landed his ship, *California Packet No. 2*, at the foot of Kimball (F) Street. Due to land title disputes with Lester Ludyah Robinson (Los Medanos Rancho), who demanded one-fourth of the property value as compensation, Kimball moved his family across the river to Kimball Island, where he established a dairy. He moved back to Antioch after the dispute was settled. Kimball died on November 18, 1879 at age 74.

BIRTHPLACE OF ANTIOCH. A stone monument was placed at the foot of Kimball (F) Street on the San Joaquin River to commemorate the site where Capt. George Washington Kimball landed his ship on September 16, 1850. His passengers became the first permanent settlers of Antioch. Also shown is a section of narrow-gauge railroad track that commemorates the Empire Railroad rail line, which extended about six miles to the coal mines south of town.

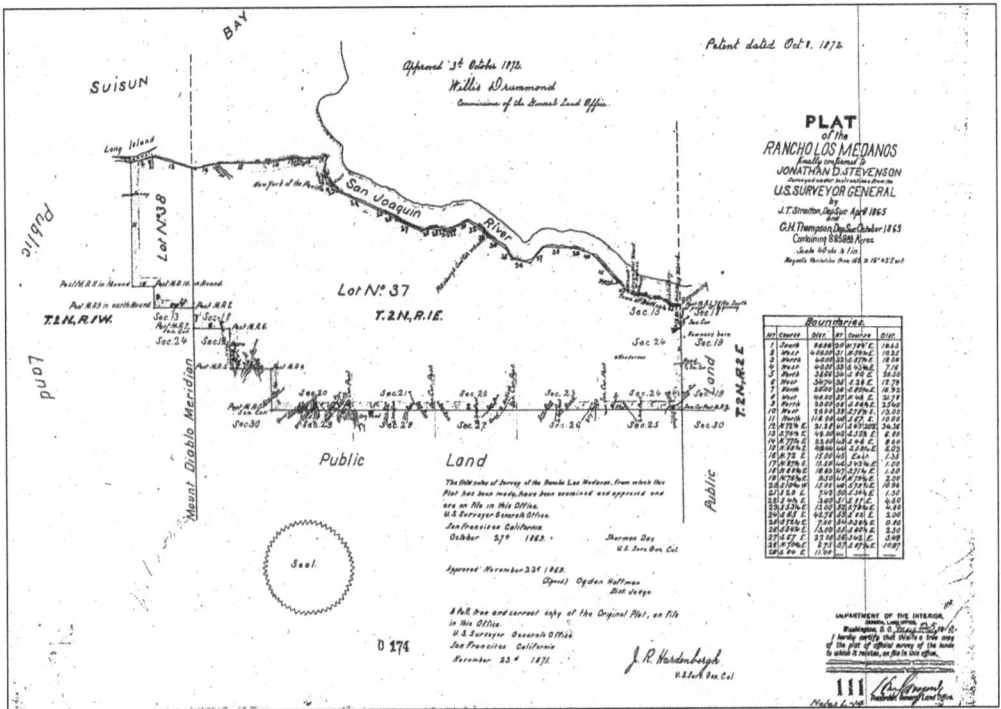

BOUNDARIES OF RANCHO LOS MEGANOS AND RANCHO LOS MEDANOS. The town of Antioch—"Distillery Wharf" on this map (plat) dated October 3, 1872—is just west of the vertical line, which is the eastern border of the Rancho Los Medanos, owned by Lester Ludyah Robinson. East of the vertical line is Rancho Los Meganos. This map defined all the land title disputes between W. W. Smith, Captain Kimball, Roswell Hard, and Lester Ludyah Robinson.

THOMAS GAINS. An emancipated slave, Thomas Gains came to Antioch in the 1860s and worked as a laborer on the Antioch dock (City Wharf). He also tended the altar of First Congregational Church. He is pictured here second from left of the horse, in front of the wagon.

BRICK HOME. Living in a small brick shed on the west side of Distillery Wharf (Jost Distillery), Thomas Gains was the only black resident of Antioch between 1860 and the 1940s. In those years, an ordinance prohibited blacks from remaining in town after dusk.

EARLIEST KNOWN PHOTOGRAPH OF ANTIOCH. This photograph was taken in the late 1860s, looking north from the corner of Main and Wyatt (I and Second) Streets. The Wilkening Saloon, operated by Fred Wilkening between 1864 to 1873, is the first building on the left. (Courtesy of Charles Bohakel.)

Two

A COMMUNITY IS BORN

In the earliest days of our community, life was hard, amenities were nonexistent, and the constant primary issue for the community was water. Although the town was settled on the banks of the San Joaquin River, the water wasn't suitable for drinking on a year-round basis. Low flows during the summer allowed salt water to move upstream from San Francisco Bay. In the beginning, citizens tried dikes, water wheels, windmills, and a reservoir for the dry season. Wells in the community were notoriously brackish, most of them germ-infested, as they had been dug too close to the privies in town. This led to years of community illness.

In 1875, the board of trustees ordered seven wells bored, and reserved all water rights in the area for the new city. Women walked to the wells daily and carried back the water needed for home use. In 1876, contractor William H. Dearien erected a 30,000-gallon water tank to supply water to the Empire Railroad. This was the first of many water projects.

Many other issues helped to make Antioch a true community. City services grew to include police protection and volunteer firemen. Future services would include parks and street paving and maintenance. Laws were enacted, one of which prohibited livestock on the wooden sidewalks. Other laws regulated business and activity of the Chinese community.

Early on, the town was known for its gambling halls and saloons. Lester L. Robinson, owner of Los Medanos Rancho, encouraged churches to build by offering them the title to lots. Churches have long been a part of the history of Antioch.

Antioch has been in the forefront throughout the history of Contra Costa County as the first city to incorporate, first to build a union high school, and one of the first to build a Carnegie library. It is now the third-largest city, behind Richmond and Concord, of the county's 19 cities.

—Compiled by Elizabeth Rimbault

ROSWELL BUTLER HARD. Elected as a Contra Costa county supervisor from 1866 to 1868, Hard was elected sheriff in 1867 and 1869 and held both jobs concurrently. An influential businessman in Antioch, Hard owned six lots and built his large two-story brick house on Front (First) Street. It was considered one of the handsomest and most costly houses in the county and served as the meeting place of the first board of trustees of the newly incorporated City of Antioch on March 2, 1872. At this meeting, Hard was elected president (mayor).

HARD HOUSE. Built in 1869 of bricks from Antioch's first brick factory, the house, now owned by the City of Antioch, still stands at 815 First Street. The Hard House is the first building in the city to be recorded on the National Registry of Historic Places.

THOMAS NEWINGTON WILLS. Wills arrived in Antioch in 1866, farmed 280 acres, and served on the first Antioch Board of Trustees, later serving as president. He is credited with developing the land south of Tenth Street.

T. N. Wills

Thomas Newington Wills arrived in Antioch in 1866, farmed 280 acres and served on first Antioch Board of Trustees, later as mayor of city —Photo by Bill Tomheim

WILLS HOME. The Wills family is pictured on the front balcony of their home, which still stands today on Ninth Street. The daughter, Helen Wills Moody, became a tennis champion and won at Wimbledon. She lived in Berkeley.

WATER CART. In 1875, the women of the community had to walk daily to one of the seven new wells, fill a water pail, and carry it home for the day's use. Those who could afford it paid the water-cart man to bring fresh water to their home to fill their cisterns during the dry season.

WATER TANK. Originally built in 1876 for the Empire Railroad, this tank, located at Fifth and F Streets, also supplied water to the residents of Antioch. In 1878, W. W. Belshaw received a franchise to lay pipes to serve individual homes directly from the water tank. The city replaced the original water tank with twin tanks at the turn of the century. In 1902, due to the pressure brought by the newly formed Woman's Club of Antioch, the community's first comprehensive water and sewer system was built, with water delivered to every home.

ANTIOCH'S ORIGINAL CITY HALL. Built in the 1860s, this two-story wooden building housed the town council chambers on the upper floor and the volunteer fire company equipment on the lower floor. The jail was located next door. Upon completion of a new city hall, the original was demolished by the Donlon family, who constructed a new building fronting on Third Street that housed the Antioch Ice and Fuel Company. The jail building was retained as an ice house/ offices until its demolition in 1981.

TOM SHINE, CITY MARSHAL. Shine was one of the earliest to serve the community. Until 1930, police services consisted of a day officer and a night watchman.

CITY BAND, C. 1900. Complete with uniforms and signs, this band consisted of Tip O'Brien, bass drum; Steve Cleaves, cymbals; Harvey Perry, baritone, D. McKellips, cornet and leader; John Donlon, tenor; Ed Wolcott, cornet; Elmer Page, alto; Dike Joslin, tenor; Robert Wall, tuba; and Nat Cleaver, drum.

VOLUNTEER FIRE DEPARTMENT HOSE TEAM, C. 1910. Pictured, from left to right, are (first row) Stone Glass, Charlie W. Taylor, Ralph Smith, and C. Bullock; (second row) Don Couray, G. Upton, Paul Ohlen, Jack Huley, and H. Wilcox; (third row) Pete Donlon, Ferd Stamm, and Jim Donlon. To gain and maintain teamwork, speed, and efficiency in getting to and fighting fires, community volunteer fire departments competed in hose-cart races. The annual summer event also provided entertainment to citizens.

24

PALACE HOTEL RAZING. In 1926, the Palace Hotel was torn down to make room for the El Campanil Theatre. A large section of the Chinese tunnel, pictured here lined with brick, was exposed. This portion was filled in and closed, but remnants of the tunnels still exist in other buildings.

AH YOUNG. A well-known resident, Ah Young was a Chinese gardener who grew a successful business selling vegetables door to door and shipping the excess to San Francisco and Stockton by ferryboat. His garden, located in the marsh behind the current Antioch Historical Society Museum, is now part of the Dow Wetlands. The original oil painting below, by Nichole Coggiola of Antioch, is on display in the Antioch Historical Society Museum.

MCKELLIPS FAMILY AND HOME. Annie "Nan" McKellips lived in the family home on Sixth Street. Her family converted the home into a boardinghouse tended by Nan.

SENATOR C. M. BELSHAW

THE BELSHAW MANSION. At 705 E Street, this home was constructed for state senator Charles M. Belshaw and his wife, Miriam. The first Mrs. Belshaw suffered from melancholy and committed suicide in the upstairs bedroom. The home was later sold to state assemblyman Robert Easley, then to the Baldocchis, who divided it into apartments for family members. The home has since been restored to its original configuration by current owners Tom and Bari Costello.

FUNERAL CORTEGE. Early pioneers Henry and Charlotte Heidorn accompany their deceased daughter, Emma Amelia, past the Trembath Ranch to her final resting place at the Oakview Cemetery in June 1896.

PALLBEARERS. This funeral procession is en route to the old God's Acre Cemetery located between Williams and Knapp (Eighth and Ninth) Streets on Boobar (G) Street. Women were frequently pallbearers for other women or children.

LAW ENFORCEMENT RECORD. Richard Veale became the longest-serving sheriff in U.S. history. His tenure ran from 1894 through 1934, spanning 40 years. Elected county treasurer in 1934, he died in office in 1937 at the age of 73. The Veale Building is located on Second Street.

SGT. RICHARD H. TREMBATH, CHP. Serving as a motorcycle officer in the 1930s, Sgt. Richard H. Trembath was one of the officers chosen to lead dignitaries across the Oakland–San Francisco Bay Bridge for the 1937 opening. While he was returning to his home in Albany, his motorcycle collided with an automobile, and he was killed instantly. Antioch businesses closed for the day of his funeral.

SECOND CITY HALL. Built in 1919 of brick faced with plaster to look like stone blocks, this edifice was located on the northwest corner of Third and H Streets. All city offices, including fire and police departments, were housed here for 30 years before the fire department moved in 1960 and the police department moved in 1965. The building continued to house city offices until the opening of the new city hall in 1981.

HOSE TEAM, C. 1920. Pictures are C. A. Sweeney, Tiny Rodgers, Donald Nelson, Lino Arata, John Roberts, and Art Ranki. In 1904, the Woman's Club of Antioch purchased the hose cart, housed in the rear of the city hall, for $400. The city had not appropriated any funds for equipment since the 1871 fire.

CHARLES A. SWEENEY. The city council authorized a four-man paid police force in 1930, with Sweeney as police chief. The council, having hired its first paid fireman in 1925 after its purchase of a Ford-chassis chemical truck, hired Sweeney as its second paid fireman in 1930. Sweeney shepherded the fire department through many years as a mostly volunteer band.

CHANGING OF THE GUARD. C. A. Sweeney turns over leadership of the Antioch Fire Department to John "Bud" Grangnelli in the late 1940s.

WATER LINES. Water lines were laid out Lone Tree Way to the reservoir to provide storage of water pumped from the San Joaquin River during salt-free periods. Today Antioch is still the only waterfront community licensed to pull water from the river.

SEWER LINES. During the Depression, the Works Progress Administration assisted both workers and the city by helping to lay new sewer lines and replace earlier, wooden water lines in the downtown area.

CORNERSTONE OF 1919 CITY HALL. Once the cornerstone was removed, it took four days to take down the walls of old city hall, despite its 62 years of wear and tear. Dedicated on December 5, 1981, a new three-story city hall with adjacent council chambers occupied 34,000 square feet and was built at a cost of $3.8 million.

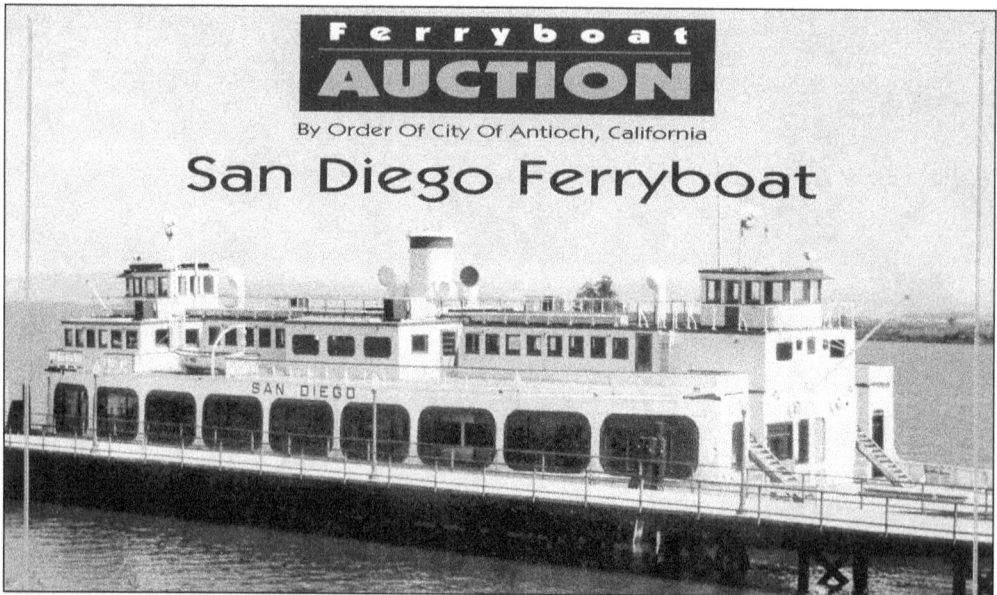

THE AUTO FERRY SAN DIEGO. The ferry was operated in Southern California between San Diego and Coronado Island. Towed from Canada to Antioch in 1986, it was moored at the Antioch fishing pier while undergoing renovations. The *San Diego* became the city's biggest controversy in the late 1980s and early 1990s. Auctioned off in 1991 for $132,500, it was towed to Sacramento for a never-completed conversion into a restaurant.

34

HENRY HEIDORN HOME. Located at 215 East Fourth (Marsh Street), this home was purchased by Henry Heidorn in 1904. Heidorn and his wife, Charlotte, retired there after farming in the Lone Tree/Neroly area.

JOHN ROSWALTER HOME. This home is located on the north side of Sixth Street, near the corner of B Street. Both the Heidorn home and the Rosswalter home were once maternity homes prior to the building of a general hospital. When it was first used as a maternity home, 106 Sixth Street was the personal residence of Dr. Diggins.

THE DOCTOR AND THE BOY. This local doctor, believed to be Dr. Nevius, made his house calls in this horse-drawn buggy, accompanied by a boy of about eight or nine years of age. The boy was Verne Roberts, who grew up to be the three-time mayor of Antioch.

SIXTH STREET, ANTIOCH COMMUNITY HOSPITAL. The rear emergency entrance of the Sixth Street hospital was most frequently seen by its patients. In this older home that was repeatedly expanded, the far-rear rooms adjacent to the ramp were the emergency room and the labor or birthing room. The hospital closed on February 7, 1967. The original home was built by Dr. Fred Nevius and later converted into a hospital.

GROUND BREAKING FOR DELTA MEMORIAL HOSPITAL, 1966. Turning the earth the old-fashioned way is Lew Silvera. Located on the site of the Hines family's wheat ranch in South Antioch, the new hospital opened its doors on February 7, 1967.

CARNEGIE LIBRARY. In 1913, the Woman's Club of Antioch surrendered all books and materials from their lending library to the newly formed Contra Costa County Library District. After purchasing a lot, they pursued and received the first Carnegie Library grant in Contra Costa County. In 1915, the lot and grant were given to the library district for the construction of the Antioch Free Library. This branch still stands today as 1 of only 2 remaining in Contra Costa County, and 1 of 87 still standing of the 144 built in California.

AIMEE-MINNIE. "The 30-foot python reportedly seen several times near the City of Antioch is shown caught in effigy Tuesday, November 13, 1934," read the caption in the *Antioch Daily Ledger*. Created from old inner tubes, the fake snake, operated by ropes, would be laid across a dark road waiting for its next victim. Unsuspecting motorists voiced their surprise and shock when catching sight of this huge creature as revealed in the dim headlights of the times. "The hoax of Antioch" was revealed after its supposed capture.

Three

CHURCHES AND ORGANIZATIONS

Religion has played a great part in the history and growth of Antioch, from its first viewing by the padres who accompanied the Spanish explorers, to its founding by itinerant preachers and naming after the biblical town of Antioch.

Many families can trace their church membership back to the earliest of churches in the area. The fellowship and security of their faith has guided them through the years. Although many of the buildings have come and gone, the membership is still going strong, and their faith has led them to take on the responsibility of helping to care for their community. From providing schools to feeding the homeless, the members of the churches of Antioch prove that a church is not just a building.

Organizations established soon after the founding of the community played their own part in the growth of the area. One of the earliest was the Masonic Lodge in 1865. The ladies of the Woman's Club of Antioch, established in 1902, were not shy when it came to raising funds and the public consciousness regarding civic issues. Many of their projects led to elections that provided funding for needed public improvements, including schools.

Responsibility is a key word in describing the many activities sponsored by the organizations that have existed since the earliest days of the community. Whether they be church-affiliated, youth character-building, sports-oriented, or fraternal, they have all found a place here and taken on a responsibility for the community. Whatever their focus, organizations have been making a difference since Antioch's beginning.

—Compiled by Carold Ann Davis

ORIGINAL CATHOLIC CHURCH. In 1864, the first Catholic mass was celebrated by Fr. Vincente Vinyes in the home of John Mulhare, northwest of downtown. Later that year, Fr. Thomas O'Neill supervised the building of the first Catholic church, a small wooden building that seated about 100 people. Twelve pews were added in 1870, when the building was enlarged by 16 feet. At first, priests from the Benicia Priory traveled to Antioch for mass every other Sunday, and, eventually, every Sunday. Holy Rosary, first a mission of St. Catherine's parish in Martinez, became a parish in 1874. Fr. Patrick Callaghan served as pastor from 1874 to 1888 and from 1893 to 1902.

HOLY ROSARY CATHOLIC CHURCH. This church, built in 1905 with locally produced brick and sandstone, fronted Seventh Street at G Street. The towers contained bells and a choir loft. After a new church was built on A Street, the original site lay empty for years, except for a community garden, because of reversionary clauses Robinson had placed in his deeds. Elizabeth Rimbault located the last heirs to the Robinson estate in the 1980s to clear the title to the land. This eventually allowed the construction of an assisted-living housing project for senior citizens on the site.

HOLY ROSARY INTERIOR. The interior of Holy Rosary Catholic Church, shown in this postcard from the 1920s, measured 120 feet in length, 60 feet wide, and 30 feet high, with a seating capacity of 400. Dedication was delayed until June 3, 1906, because of the 1906 earthquake.

FIRST CONGREGATIONAL CHURCH. Founded on June 12, 1865, the congregation held meetings in city hall and the schoolhouse at Utter and Boobar Streets. The original building, constructed on the corner of Utter and Kimball (Sixth and F) Streets, was dedicated in 1869 and demolished in 1891 to build a new church on the same site.

1891 FIRST CONGREGATIONAL CHURCH BUILDING. Dedicated in 1891, the new church was built at a cost of almost $6,000 in about four months time. The year 1932 saw the removal of the church steeple as far as the belfry, due to deteriorating framework. Although the congregation moved in 1968, both the congregation and the building are still active. The building is the oldest continuously used church building remaining in the city of Antioch.

CONGREGATION. Members of the First Congregational Church, pictured on the church steps after Sunday services in the early 1900s, include Henry and Charlotte Heidorn and granddaughter Marie Heidorn. Mr. Heidorn served as a deacon in the church.

Methodist Church, Antioch, Ca[...]

ANTIOCH METHODIST CHURCH. While it first fronted on G Street next door to the Woman's Club clubhouse and featured a vestibule, the church was later picked up, turned to the right, moved to the back of the lot, and set down facing Sixth Street. The front portico of the church was lost during the move. The vacant lot created on the corner was used as a gas station for many years and is now a visitor parking lot. After the Methodists sold it, the building was occupied by a furniture store and an art gallery. Today it is once again used as a church. In the background on the right is the steeple of the First Congregational Church, before it was taken down in 1932.

LODGE NO. 175, FREE AND ACCEPTED MASONS. An organizational meeting was held in Somersville on May 8, 1865, for a new lodge to be established in Antioch. Members included coal miners, farmers, butchers, carpenters, shoemakers, merchants, and attorneys. All in all, 15 Masons signed the petition to establish the lodge. The first meeting was held on June 17, 1865. Due to the difficulty of traveling from place to place, especially at night, meetings were held in keeping with the full of the moon. The lodge predated newspapers (the *Antioch Ledger*'s first edition was March 30, 1870) and railroads (Southern Pacific came to town in 1878) and continues in operation over 140 years since its inception.

43

Bank Building, Antioch, Cal.

WOMAN'S CLUB OF ANTIOCH, 1902. Meeting at first in their homes, the Woman's Club planned for the future by purchasing a lot on G Street in 1906 for $200 from Henry Fuller Beede. Still unable to build in 1907, the ladies rented rooms above the first Bank of Antioch on Second Street. In March 1910, the ladies voted to construct a one-room clubhouse on their lot and sold cardboard shingles for 10¢ each for the building fund. Festivities marked its opening in September 1910. Although unable to vote yet, the Woman's Club of Antioch was credited with the following in the downtown area: oiling or paving of the first four streets; the first water system to individual homes; the first sewer system, and the outlaw of privies in downtown.

MARGARET MCNULTY BEEDE. Henry Fuller Beede's wife was a founding member of the Woman's Club of Antioch.

DEGREE OF POCOHANTAS, APRIL 7, 1910. The Order of Red Men, a patriotic fraternity chartered by Congress in 1813, is a nonprofit organization devoted to inspiring a greater love for the United States of America and the principles of American liberty. Among its earliest members were the Sons of Liberty, who were responsible for the Boston Tea Party. The Degree of Pocahontas was created for women on January 15, 1887, drawing on the legend of its namesake and the virtues of her life.

ANCIENT EGYPTIAN ORDER OF SCIOTS. Established in San Francisco in 1905 as a social club for Masons, this organization fostered friendship, fellowship, cooperation, and the spirit of boosting one another through unity in all things.

IOOF Officers, 1950.
Instituted January 11, 1869, the San Joaquin Lodge No. 151, IOOF, has met on the second floor of the building once known as Union Hall since its completion in 1878. To meet construction costs for the building on the southeast corner of Third and H Streets, the IOOF paid half of the total cost of $4,347.44 and the Masonic Lodge paid the other half. The two organizations also equally shared ownership of the Masons and Odd Fellows Cemetery.

Mizpah Rebekah Lodge No. 102. The IOOF became the first national fraternity to include women in their organization with the adoption of the Rebekah Degree in 1851. Their purpose was to promote charitable works. Here the Rebekah's float awaits its turn as the 1911 Fourth of July parade forms on First Street in front of the Santa Fe Railroad Depot.

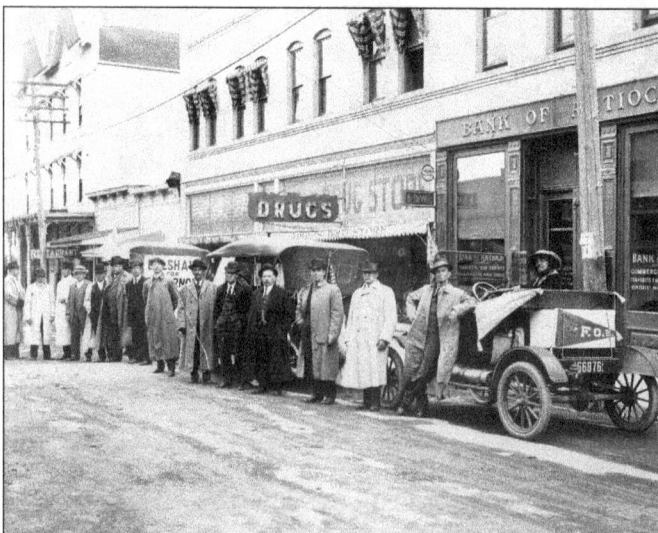

Fraternal Order of Eagles. Pictured on Wyatt (Second) Street, this 1914 gathering of Eagles preparing for an outing includes (in the white duster) constable Charles Sweeney, who later served as police chief.

46

NATIVE SONS OF THE GOLDEN WEST. At the dedication of the John Marsh home as a historical monument in 1934, members of the General Winn Parlor No. 39 included, from left to right, Dick Trembath, Jack Welch, Richard Uren, R. R. Veale, and Jud Biglow.

HOLY ROSARY YOUNG LADIES INSTITUTE DRILL TEAM. The Holy Rosary drill team members pictured here are, from left to right, (standing, left) Josephine Rubio; (first row, kneeling) Mamie Frediani, unidentified, Stella Iacona, Bruna Checchi, Edwina Waters, Betty Rose, Marie Jacobson, Violet Renzenbrink, Margaret San Martin, and Mary Rodriguez; (second row) Frieda Marchetti, Jane Reis, Norma Reis, Marie Viera, Leviane Reis, Lydia Banti, Ann Nabas, Florinda Marks, Nikki Vramis, and Joan Courtney.

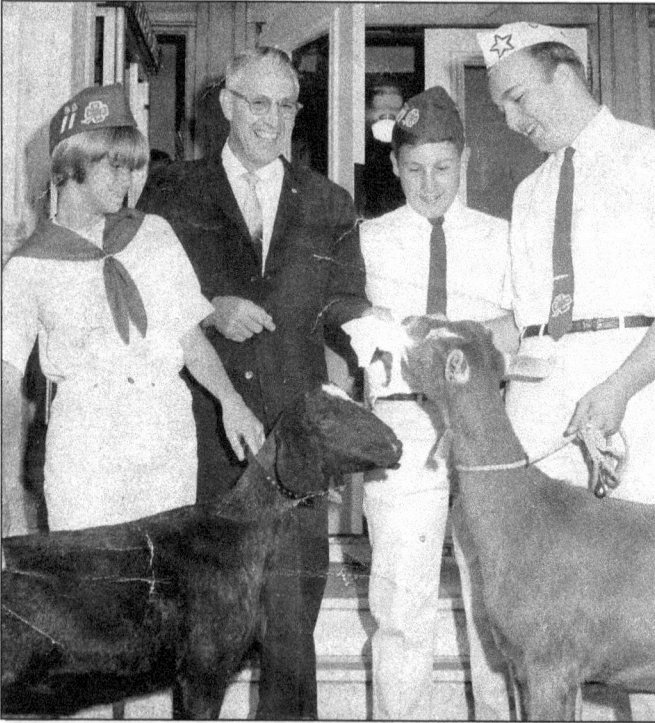

4-H CLUB MEMBERS. Mayor Verne Roberts greets 4-H members Cindy Hiebert, David Stitt, Jeff Huffaker, and their special project goats on the steps of Antioch City Hall. East County youths have made the most of the opportunity to showcase their stock projects with the county fairgrounds located in Antioch.

DELTA DRIFTERS. Uril "Compy" Compomizzo, with his wife, Anna, organized the Delta Drifters Square Dance Club in the 1960s.

CONTRA COSTA FAIR PARADE. The Contra Costa Fair, a highlight of the summer, hosted a parade that involved and entertained the entire community. Hundreds of citizens lined the parade route, arriving early with their chairs and lunches to get the best seats to watch the floats assembled by local organizations, bands, drill teams, and military units. Participants included the sheriff's mounted posse and Spanish senoritas with polished silver saddles and beautiful gowns draped over their horses' flanks. Then came the clowns with their brooms. The judges' stand was usually located at the corner of G and Second Streets. This 1957 photograph shows John Viera driving his carriage carrying Alice Webster, Kate Heidorn Trembath, Emma Lynn, Etta Forest, and Anna I. Beede.

THE CLAMPERS. E Clampus Vitus, Joaquin Murrieta Chapter 13, constructed this monument in front of the Riverview Union High School (Antioch Historical Society Museum) to commemorate its designation on the Registry of Historic Sites for both the state and nation. The monument was unveiled on November 4, 2000, the 89th anniversary of the school opening. A dual celebration was held with the symbolic "burning of the mortgage," with city officials and historical society members gathered around.

HEIDORN-TREMBATH LEGACY. Phyllis Trembath-Hiebert and her sister Kathy Trembath-Lescure point out great-granddad Henry Heidorn's name on the original 1912 cornerstone of the Riverview Union High School. Kathy Lescure's husband and son are pictured here with their five granddaughters, part of the legacy of a pioneer family that also included Richard J. Trembath, Antioch and East County representative on the Contra Costa County Board of Supervisors for 25 years. His name, as supervisor, was inscribed on the original Antioch Bridge, the Oakland–San Francisco Bay Bridge, and the Caldecott Tunnel.

LAST MAN OF THE LAST MAN'S CLUB. An organization of early businessmen, who promoted the downtown merchants and businesses, passed this magnum of champagne around through the presidents of the organization. The last man living was to open the bottle of champagne and toast the memories of all former members. Last man Robert Swain stated that he had no friends left to drink with and never opened the bottle. After his death in 1994, Swain's widow donated the unopened bottle and club records to the Antioch Historical Society, where it is on display in the museum.

Four

SCHOOL DAYS

The new settlement of Antioch was hardly formed when its founders realized that along with the establishment of the city boundaries and an early form of government, the next most important task to accomplish was the building of a school. Although Captain Kimball appointed a woman named Martha Douglas to be the first-known teacher in town, her unstable health soon made it clear that she would not be able to do the job. The captain then appointed his daughter Adelia Barrett Kimball as the first official teacher in the fledgling Antioch school system. The galley of an abandoned ship was set up on the corner of Sixth and G Streets in the fall of 1850, and it was here that Miss Kimball assumed the duties of teacher when she herself was only 12 years old. Many of her students were older than she, but this was not uncommon in those days.

Mr. James Cruickshank became the next teacher, and the school moved to a small one-room house on E Street. The 1865–1866 report of the County Superintendent of Common Schools reported that Antioch had a census count of 86 children, 71 of whom attended school. A teacher received $421.21 per year, plus room and board.

A more suitable and permanent two-story brick building was erected on G Street between Fifth and Sixth Streets in 1869 with funds subscribed by the people of Antioch. It was replaced in 1890 by a new, two-story wooden structure known as the Antioch Grammar School, which had many modern innovations. The original Antioch Primary School, later renamed John Muir School, was the next school building on this site and remained in use as a school until 1962 when it was closed to students because it did not meet state requirements for earthquake safety. The building was utilized as a district library and for storage until it was finally demolished in 1986. With the building of the Antioch Unified School District Administration Building, this historic site has served the children of Antioch since 1869.

The early settlers of the Lone Tree and Deer Valley areas south of town also realized the importance of educating their children and so applied to the county board of education to establish the Lone Tree District.

The Live Oak School, which was located east of Bridgehead Road, was also a one-room school used for residents in that area. Notes from the W. W. Smith diary indicate he built or worked on many of the small school buildings throughout the area.

In 1891, a special election (later declared to be illegal) was held by the county school board to decide on establishing a high school in Antioch. Approved by 12 of 16 of the outlying areas, the new high school, located in the second story of the new grammar school building, opened in September 1891, with Granville P. Foster as its first principal. The 16 upper-grade students came from Byron, Bay Point, Willow Pass, and the Lone Tree area. These students attended classes until they were able to pass a battery of tests that earned them a diploma. Some of these students from the Lone Tree and Deer Valley areas found it necessary to live at the home of Judge Hartley on the corner of Fourth and G Streets during the week because of the difficulty in traveling such a long distance in the wet winters.

In 1903, the Riverview Union High School was established. Classes were again held on the G Street site, with students attending from the Black Diamond (Pittsburg), Antioch, Somersville and Carbondale Districts. The Lone Tree and Live Oak Districts soon joined them. In 1907, the first class of seven graduated. In 1908, a special election passed providing funding for the construction of a union high school. Students from both the Pittsburg and Antioch areas attended classes there from 1911 until 1922, when the Pittsburg School District was formed and those students withdrew from Riverview Union High School District. Antioch then formed the Antioch–Live Oak District, and students continued to attend the Riverview Union High School until a bond issue was passed in 1931 and a new Antioch High School was built on D Street. A larger Antioch High School, built in August 1954 on East Eighteenth Street, opened in 1955 and is still in use.

—Compiled by Phyllis Hiebert

ANTIOCH'S FIRST PERMANENT TEACHER. The first classes were taught by 12-year-old Adelia Kimball, daughter of Captain Kimball. In 1855, Miss Kimball attended Rincon Point School No. 1 in San Francisco. She graduated from San Francisco Normal School in January, 1863. She married John Schott in September 1863. They first resided on Kimball Island, where her husband first cultivated asparagus. After receiving her own diploma and marrying, she never taught school again, as was the custom in those times.

ANTIOCH GRAMMAR SCHOOL, 1869. Erected in 1869, this two-story brick building measured 32 by 50 feet. Funded mostly by subscription, the value of the school property for 1869–1870 was recorded as $4,000. Occupied until 1890, this building and several additional wooden structures were demolished to make way for the new school.

ANTIOCH GRAMMAR SCHOOL, 1890. This two-story, wooden-frame building, erected in 1890 on the same site as the first grammar school at a cost of $15,000, measured 99 by 89 feet. With separate entrances for boys and girls, the building served students until it was demolished in 1926.

BELSHAW THEATER. Located on the second floor of the Belshaw Building in downtown Antioch, the theater is pictured here set up for an Eagles memorial service in 1910. The theater served as the location of graduation ceremonies for the Riverview Union High School, as well as for high school plays and basketball games as the new Riverview Union High School was built without a gymnasium.

ANTIOCH PRIMARY SCHOOL, 1933. Students known to be in this photograph, in no particular order, are Chris Laurentzen, Uril Compomizzo, Reno Bastinelli, Joe Nabis, Tony Gonsalves, Jack Cone, David Moore, Candalerio Cabrera, ? Parune, Butch Rodriguez, Adolpho Najaro, Harry Harris, Lidia Banti, Louella Moore, Mary Moura. The young man on the extreme right, in the dark sweater and knee pants, is future congressman Jerome Waldie.

LONE TREE SCHOOL, C. 1896. A one-room school was built sometime in the 1870s on the north side of Lone Tree Way. Located across from what is now known as Heidorn Ranch Road, the school served the farms and ranches southeast of town until absorbed into the Antioch Unified District in the 1960s. Many of the early Lone Tree corridor settlers' descendants attended this school, and some returned later to teach. Florine McFarlan taught at the school for 25 years. One of the early trustees was Henry Heidorn, a pioneer rancher in the area. Teacher Kate Heidorn (beginning of third row, wearing hat) and students from Williamson, McFarlan, Lynch, Gann, Golden, and Loryea families are pictured here around 1896.

LIVE OAK SCHOOL. The Contra Costa Gazette reported on May 12, 1883, that plans were being made for the formation of the Live Oak School District. The school was to be located on property halfway between the Oakley area and the town of Antioch at the corner of Live Oak Avenue and Highway 4. A petition was circulated during the summer of 1921 to consolidate the Live Oak and Antioch Districts. A special election held in the fall of 1921 resulted in the formation of the Antioch–Live Oak School District. It would be a number of years before the district would be renamed again as the Antioch Unified School District. After the building was no longer used as a school, it housed the Grange and the Farm Bureau. Today it is owned by a church.

Riverview Union High School, Antioch, Cal.

RIVERVIEW UNION HIGH SCHOOL. In 1908, in response to a state mechanism that allowed funding for union districts, a special election was passed to approve the construction of the Riverview Union High School. To end a dispute between Pittsburg and Antioch over the location, C. A. Hooper stepped in and donated land at Fourth and Somersville, between the two cities, for the construction. Built in 1910 and opening to teach the first class on November 4, 1911, Riverview Union High School was the first high school constructed in Contra Costa County. Following graduation in 1931, the remaining students were moved to the new Antioch High School on D Street and the school closed. The building was then occupied by the Bureau of Reclamation during the design and construction of the Central Valley Project, with the Contra Costa Canal being the first stage of the project. It was purchased in 1947 by the Fibreboard Corporation for Fibreboard Research. The Riverview Fire Protection District acquired the building in 1965 for its headquarters and abandoned it in 1994. The Antioch Historical Society purchased the building in 1999 and maintains a museum on the site.

LIBERTY BOND DRIVE, 1917. Standing on the northwest steps of the back of the Riverview Union High School, these Boy Scouts are ready to do their part in selling liberty bonds.

56

RIVERVIEW UNION HIGH SCHOOL TRACK TEAM, 1924. Members of the team included, from left to right, (first row) Stanley Carpenter, Phil Nash, Abie "Jimmy" Dixon, Tom Hines, John Wood, Kenneth "Wally" Rooker, and Don Graham Kirk; (second row) Gene Doherty, Willard Ridings, "Pop" Ellis, Edward "Grub" Smith, Ham Holliday, Francis "Babe" Webster, and Mr. A. V. Carleton (shop teacher and coach).

CLASS AT WOMAN'S CLUB OF ANTIOCH. Records show that the Woman's Club of Antioch clubhouse was leased to the school district from 1920 through 1922 to ease overcrowding of the Antioch Grammar School across the street. Note that the hats worn by three of the girls were the World War I army hats of their fathers or uncles, worn sideways.

MUSIC LESSONS. This photograph taken between 1885 and 1890 shows that music was seen as a cultural necessity in the lives of children and families.

Left to Right: Unknown, Unknown, Elizabeth Hufhines, David Heredia and Elizabeth Fidalgo. Spring 1942, in front of the Woman's Club of Antioch's Clubhouse. Donated by Eleanor (Hufhines) O'Donnell.

SPRING OF 1942. While choral music was always taught in the primary schools, instrumental music lessons were considered a frill for the school district of the 1940s. Therefore, Carmen Dragon, the famous conductor who was born and schooled in Antioch, received no instrumental music training from the schools in his primary years. During this time, the Woman's Club of Antioch opened their clubhouse to after-school instrumental music lessons.

ANTIOCH HIGH SCHOOL ON D STREET. Opened for classes in 1932, this school was the first high school (9th through 12th grades) solely owned and constructed by the Antioch–Live Oak Unified School District, the Union District having been dissolved years before. In 1954, a new Antioch Senior High School was built on East Eighteenth Street, west of G Street, and this building became the Antioch Junior High School for grades seven through nine. In 1965, the original brick building was torn down due to earthquake damage, and the new Antioch Jr. High School (now called Antioch Middle School) was constructed in its place.

ANTIOCH HIGH SCHOOL CHAMPIONSHIP BAND, 1942. The band is pictured in front of the entrance of the D Street Antioch High School. Band members include Carmen Dragon.

WESTERN DRESS DAY AT ANTIOCH HIGH SCHOOL. This event was right up there in popularity with the Sock Hop and Senior Ditch Day. The photograph was probably taken in the Senior Court, located in a courtyard in the center of the building. Only seniors could enter the courtyard, naturally.

ANTIOCH HIGH STUDENTS, C. 1942. Were the soldiers in this World War II jeep recruiters or helping with a bond drive? Pictured, from left to right, are (first row) Mrs. Woodward (teacher), Betty Rose, Hazel Peres, unidentified, and Mary Vargo; (second row) Harold Hood, Walter Eells, and unidentified soldiers.

ANTIOCH HIGH SCHOOL, EAST EIGHTEENTH STREET. This is the architect's rendering of what the Antioch High School campus was to look like when completed. As with most construction projects, this drawing and the actual construction differ greatly. Beede Auditorium, with a seating capacity of 1,200, was the largest venue in the city when constructed and was used to stage events for various organizations. Several benefit concerts for Delta Memorial Hospital were held there that included such stars as Bob Hope, Barbara Mandrell, and Red Skelton. The building's construction came into question when several of the concrete roof beams fell from their supports in March 1980 during a drama class.

ANTIOCH GRAMMAR SCHOOL. This school was originally named Antioch Grammar School but was later torn down and reconstructed on the same site as John Fremont Elementary School.

61

ANTIOCH GRAMMAR SCHOOL. Students enjoy the balmy spring air with a maypole dance in the 1950s. All elementary schools celebrated May Day with demonstrations of ribbon and folk dancing, including well-rehearsed maypole dances. The practice was discontinued as the cold war escalated.

NELLIE BEEDE KELLEY, MAY 14, 1966. Nellie Kelley was the only representative of the 1907 graduating class of Riverview Union High School, prior to the construction of the Riverview Union High School building, to attend the combined high school reunion for classes from 1907 through 1936. Here Mayor Verne Roberts, a graduate of the class of 1932, presents her with roses.

Five

FARMING AND LAND CONSERVATION

To fully appreciate the way farming developed in the Antioch area, it is important to know about the weather conditions and soil problems the early settlers were up against. The climate in the area fluctuated, from years of very little rain to years of more than adequate rainfall. The spring brought green grass and wildflowers to the plains and hills of the area north and east of Mount Diablo, but, as spring ended and the drying north winds swept across the San Joaquin River, the wild oats, poppies, lupine, and other indigenous plants withered and died until the next seasons rains called them forth again. There was no irrigation early on, and the farmer sowed the grain and hoped that the rains would be timely to sprout the seed.

The earliest settlers first saw sand dunes next to the river that were extensive in some areas. There were good-sized streams that flowed down from the foothills and Marsh Creek area, and swampy areas filled with tules, pussy willows, and other forms of swamp grass that melded into the delta as far as the eye could see. The area was thickly covered with California live oaks and scrub brush that all needed to be cleared before crops could be planted.

The earliest farmers came to the area in the 1850s and 1860s. Many of the properties were acquired by land grant from the federal government. The major crops in the early days were oats and hay. The harvested grain was taken to Marsh Landing for shipment down river on a scow to San Francisco. Hay from the Heidorn and other neighboring ranches was sold to the City of San Francisco to feed the horses of the Police and Fire Department.

Captain Kimball grew oats and hay on Kimball and Sherman Islands, as well as raising hogs and dairy cattle. Most of the farmers were self sufficient, as they maintained their own basic food supplies. Almost everyone had a milk cow and chickens. Some more enterprising farmers supplemented their income by selling meat and eggs to other farmers and the city dwellers of Antioch.

The Higgins, Ginochio, and Arata families were the leading cattle ranchers of the Antioch area, owning and leasing grazing lands in the southern and western portions south of Antioch.

As time went on and more property was cleared and leveled, other crops were planted. Most of the Lone Tree corridor immediately south of Antioch remained in hay and grain, with some cattle grazing. Starting at the Heidorn Ranch, apricots, peaches, and walnuts were planted. Almonds and fruit trees grew farther east on Lone Tree. Many school students will remember "cutting 'cots," which were then sulfured and dried.

Antioch ended at Tenth Street in the early days, and a dirt road (A Street) took you to Iron House Road (East Eighteenth Street), where several smaller farms were located. These farms grew almonds, walnuts, and grapes. East of Viera Lane, Manuel Viera planted grapes all the way out to Bridgehead.

The farmers shipped their crops downriver on scows and steamers. When the market price was too low, they would store their grain and hay in the warehouses that were located on the docks on Antioch's waterfront until the price was reasonable.

The Balfour Guthrie Company, a British investment firm, purchased the Marsh Ranch and brought irrigation to the entire east county, all the way to the Lone Tree area. This company also helped to develop what was called the "Market Basket of the World." Farming became easier with the addition of water to grow crops. There were many downturns through the years, and many good farmers lost their properties during the Great Depression.

—Compiled by Phyllis Heibert

TREMBATH RANCH. Richard Trembath Jr. immigrated to the United States sometime in the 1840s. His parents, aunt, and two brothers left Cornwall to follow him, and they all settled in California in late 1853. He and his brothers mined successfully in the French Gulch area. Richard married and, in 1869, came to the Antioch area, where he purchased 160 acres from a John Jessup—just one mile southeast of the fledgling city of Antioch. The road, which ran in front of the Oak Tree in this photograph, was called the Antioch Iron House Road (later the Oakley Highway, the Victory Highway, and now East Eighteenth Street). The area immediately west of this house is now Trembath Lane. The Trembaths raised hay and grain and later planted grapes, almonds, and fruit trees.

ALMOND HULLER. Harvesting the almond crop on the Trembath Ranch east of Antioch was a very labor-intensive undertaking. (Courtesy of Phyllis Trembath Hiebert.)

WELCH RANCH. John Welch, shown in his carriage, left Ireland on his own when he was only 14 years old. He eventually settled in Antioch on a ranch near the Trembath and Uren Ranches off of Hillcrest Avenue. These three pioneer families were related through marriage.

UREN RANCH. Richard Uren mined in the French Gulch area with the Trembaths. He married Phyllis Trembath, the sister of Richard Trembath Sr. The Trembath and Uren families rented and farmed "section five," which later became the Joe Prewett Ranch. The two families harvested grain together and owned a combine harvester with 14 horses at one time. Most of the farmers in the area worked together to bring the harvest to market.

ORLANDER AND BECKY PREWETT. The Prewetts, pictured here around 1900, owned as many as 40 horses and provided many of the horses bought by local farmers. The Prewett Ranch is the current home of the Prewett Community Water Park.

QUINN-JENSEN WEDDING. Margaret Quinn and Martin Jensen were married around 1910, south of Antioch proper.

Drying Fruit, Antioch, Cal.

DRYING FRUIT. The harvest included a variety of fruits and nuts.

RUCKSTUHL VINEYARDS. Joseph Ruckstuhl is pictured standing in front of his acreage, one of the largest grape vineyards in the Antioch area, located on the north side of old Highway 4, east of Bridgehead Road. This property was later sold to the Dupont Corporation, considered one of Antioch's major industrial employers.

JOE NOIA, WILLIAM GRIBBLE, AND AMOS GRAVES. Note the wicker-covered wine bottle in the foreground in this photograph from August 24, 1902. Used to ship wine, the covering protected it from both light and breakage. The Masons and Odd Fellows organizations established a cemetery on 20 acres purchased from Graves.

HINES-FITZPATRICK RANCH ON LONE TREE WAY. The teamsters/farmers had to keep control of their teams at all times because of the steep hills in some areas. There was very little flat land in the area where the grain was planted. The harvester was fitted with a braking device and the teamsters needed to be constantly aware of the next rise or fall of the territory. In very steep areas, it was necessary to have a rider on the lead horse to prevent a runaway or very bad accident. The brakeman and the driver worked closely together to keep things operating. Since the height of the grain was variable, the header operator was responsible for keeping the header at the height of the grain. This job was not for the faint of heart.

FARM EQUIPMENT, C. 1894. Machines other than harvesters were needed on the ranches and farms, such as this steam engine from the Viera ranch.

VIERA RANCH, 1894. The piece of machinery shown here, part of a hay press, was also on the Viera ranch.

LADIES ON THE HARVESTER. The ladies on the harvester in this photograph may have sewn the grain sacks closed when they were full. The needle used was about six inches long and was threaded with a heavy twine. There was a special way that the corner was twisted into what looked like an ear on each side, with 9 stitches for barley and 12 stitches for wheat running along on the top of the sack. This was done rapidly, but carefully, to be sure no grain was lost.

DRAFT TEAMS. Each farmer contributed their livestock to form huge teams. Some farmers, such as John Viera, used horses and mules but preferred mules as the leaders of the teams. Each draft animal was known by its individual name and personality.

HARVEST TEAM. Working dawn to dusk under the drying, hot sun, often trying to beat the weather during the small harvest window, aged these young men far beyond their years.

SACKED AND READY FOR SHIPMENT. What could be better than having the crop in and ready for shipment?

BILL WILLIAMSON, DRIVER. Four mules were needed to pull the 5,830-pound weight of this rig. Similar rigs from the McFarlan Ranch were hauled to the Jost Distillery on the Antioch waterfront. Bill Williamson is pictured here delivering wheat to Antioch's Santa Fe Railroad station.

SCHOONER GLEANER. When the railroads were too costly, wheat, and other grains were shipped to San Francisco by schooners such as this one.

San Francisco, *Mach 8* 1882

M̲

Bought of **W. H. Brockhoff,**

DEALER IN BEST AMERICAN

Beef, Mutton, Veal, Pork & Sausages

OF ALL KINDS, A SPECIALTY.

PETALUMA MARKET, cor. 24th and Bryant Streets.

All Orders promptly executed on the Shortest Notice and on Most Reasonable Terms.

DEMPSTER BROS., PRINTERS NO. 9 BOND ST.

PETALUMA MARKET. W. H. Brockhoff owned the Petaluma Market, located in San Francisco. The brother of Charlotte Heidorn, he would journey upriver from time to time, then travel out to the Lone Tree area to purchase, butcher, and process livestock. While there, he traveled up to the mines area to take orders and deliver meat products to the hotels and residents.

PHARCELLUS "CELLUS" BIGLOW AND HIS PRIZE BULL. The Biglow family once had a dairy on the southeast corner of Tenth and G Streets, then moved out to the end of Wilbur Avenue near Marsh Landing. There were many small commercial dairies located in Antioch and the adjoining countryside. Almost all farmers had a milk cow or two, but as the population increased, there was a need to supply milk commercially. Milk was sold to the customer in jars or tins, some of which were supplied by the customer.

MINAKER DAIRY. One of the larger dairies to deliver milk door to door was owned by the Minaker Family. When Calvin and his wife, Mabel, arrived in the Antioch area around 1902, they lived and farmed on West Island. In 1906, they purchased 20 acres on the south side of Wilbur Avenue and farmed almonds, grapes, and walnuts. They later purchased an additional 30 acres from the Gallo family.

MINAKER DAIRY COWS. In 1929, the Minakers purchased a herd of purebred Guernsey and Jersey cows. With about 30 milk cows, all named, the dairy became the primary family income. Their milk was sold in modern, sterilized bottles. The dairy continued in operation through World War II.

CENTRAL-SHUEY CREAMERY
GOLDEN STATE COMPANY, LTD.
MANUFACTURER, DISTRIBUTOR AND EXPORTER

GOLDEN STATE BRAND MILK PRODUCTS

5307 TELEGRAPH AVE.   PHONE OLYMPIC 3000
OAKLAND, CALIFORNIA

GOLDEN STATE COMPANY, LT
5307 TELEGRAPH AVE.   PHONE OLYMP
OAKLAND, CALIFORNIA

30	MR. R. J. TREMBATH	67	30	MR. R. J. TREMBATH	
	TREMBATH & FREDRICKSON			TREMBATH & FREDRIC	
603	ANTIOCH, CALIF		603	ANTIOCH, CALIF	

REMITTANCE STUB

PRODUCT	QUANTITY	$	AMOUNT	MEMO	$	AMOUNT	CUSTOME
BAL			4.38	5		4.38	30
BAL			3.60	6		3.60	30
MILK · QT ·	5		.65			.65	30
MILK · PT ·	15		1.20			1.20	30
DUE			9.83			9.83	

DETACH HERE

JULY 1931   JULY 1931

Use dairy products freely in your cooking. A little cream .. a bit of butter, greatly improve nutriment and flavor.

PLEASE DETACH THIS STUB AND MAIL WIT
REMITTANCE AS IT WILL ASSIST US IN CR
YOUR ACCOUNT PROMPTLY.
"BAL" DENOTES THE BALANCE OF A PRIOR
STILL UNPAID.
"DUE" INDICATES TOTAL AMOUNT NOW D
PAYABLE.

OTHER DAIRIES. Although the Central Shuey Dairy was in Oakland, their heifers were raised near Deer Valley and Empire Mine Roads. The crumbled remains of a very large complex of barns can still be seen at that location. In more recent times, the Burrough Brothers' Dairy, another large operation located near Knightsen, delivered milk to Antioch and all of the local schools.

Six

BUSINESS AND COMMERCE

From the very beginning, Antioch was the hub of business activity in East Contra Costa County, providing jobs, goods, and services to all the local residents, surrounding communities and industries. Initially all the goods were shipped to Antioch by river transport and then by rail. Between the community's birth and the early 1900s, several doctors made their residence in Antioch; a number of drugstores lined G and Second Streets; several general mercantile stores of good reputation were located throughout the town; lawyers and dentists occupied upper stories of buildings; and hotels and restaurants provided lodging for visitors and dining for all.

In the late 1940s, the business community, as well as the industries, experienced a period of rapid, postwar growth. New demands were placed on industries to produce consumer goods to fill orders for those goods placed by local businesses.

While the El Campanil Theater, with four little shops under its wings, was the pride of the northwest corner of the intersection of Second and G Streets, the other four corners saw many changes during this time: Famous Fashions, established in 1941 by Mr. And Mrs. S. Haas, took over the Howse Hardware building on the northeast corner; The White Fountain, established by the Jackson family, and Jensen's Department Store moved into the lower levels of the Belshaw building, on the southeast corner, while the Masonic Lodge remained upstairs; James Men's Store, established by James Davi, opened in the old Antioch Bank of Savings location on the southwest corner. In addition, The Madd Hatter Hat Shop, created by Velma Jennings, opened adjacent to James Men's Store; Leo Fontana started Antioch Stationers a little farther down Second Street in 1946, providing office supplies and business machines to the growing community; and jeweler Eugene Mayer moved his store to the east of Famous Fashions in 1948. The stores were suddenly specialized to appeal to consumer demands, as the corner of Second and G Streets was transformed from hardware and general mercantile to the fashion center of the community.

Cries of laughter from other merchants rang in the ears of businessmen that ventured out to the area of A and Eighteenth Streets with the construction of the ABC Building (Antioch Business Center) on the southwest corner of Twentieth and A Streets—the first building in town to have an elevator! Heathorn Pharmacy, founded in 1949 on the northwest corner of Twentieth and A Streets, was sold to Victor Greenwood and became Greenwood Pharmacy in 1957. The Hottertop Restaurant and a Five and Ten Cent Store were established across A Street. The southwest corner of Eighteenth and A Streets was occupied by the Enea Dairy and office building until the early 1960s when construction began on the Eastwood Shopping Center (formerly anchored by Lucky

Stores). Shortly thereafter, the Antioch Square Shopping Center (with Safeway) began construction on the northeast corner of the intersection. Several established downtown businesses moved out to these new locations, including Davi Men's Store, the Madd Hatter, Jensen's Department Store, and Rexall Drugs.

While downtown continued as a shopping area, in part thanks to the Sears Roebuck store (23,000 square feet) built in 1952 and a Montgomery Ward catalog and appliance store (established in 1957), the construction of these two shopping centers began the demise of the robust downtown commercial area. Businesses began moving out of downtown to the south, toward newer housing, and, when a major shopping mall was constructed at Somersville and Delta Fair Boulevard in the late 1960s, both Sears and Wards joined the exodus by moving to the mall. Sears became an anchor store in the new County East Mall with Mervyn's and Grants. The population was expanding and residents wanted shopping to be located closer to their new housing developments while businesses wanted to be located nearer the freeway (State Route 4) to attract business from more than one community. In the mid-1970s, Grants closed and J. C. Penney's became an anchor. In the 1980s, the mall was enclosed and Gottschalks added as a fourth anchor. The late 1990s saw J. C. Penney's leave and 2004 brought Macy's to town and a new name to the mall: Somersville Towne Center.

—Compiled by Elizabeth Rimbault

PETERSON PLOW WORKS. Nelson Peterson's blacksmith and factory produced Peterson cultivators (plows), which he invented for farming the peat soils of the delta. The building remained well into the 1970s until the land was needed to expand the city hall parking lot.

HUNTER LIVERY STABLE. An important business at the turn of the century, the livery stable served transportation needs, with horses and buggies for rent. The building that now occupies this site on G Street served as an early post office and later as a telephone exchange.

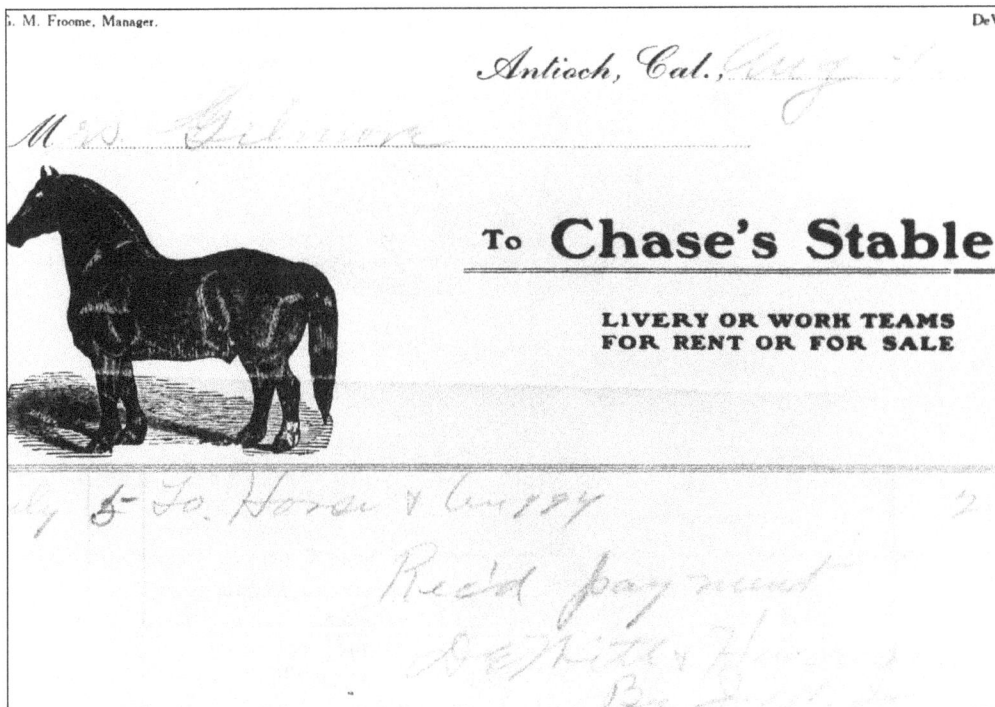

CHASE'S STABLE. Located at Brown and Main (Third and I) Streets, this stable and several other businesses were destroyed by the "Great Antioch Fire" of August 23, 1871.

BANK OF ANTIOCH. Established September 12, 1891, with S. G. Little as president, the Bank of Antioch was located on the north side of Wyatt (Second) Street until 1923, when it moved to newly constructed quarters on the northeast corner of Second and H Streets. The bank remained in this location after its merger with the Bank of America in 1934, although it eventually relocated to the northeast corner of Fourth and G Streets. The 1923 bank building now houses the Rivertown Arts Center.

ARLINGTON HOTEL. First opened in 1890 as the Dickerson Hotel, the building was located on the north side of Wyatt Street (Second) between G and H. This grand hotel of Antioch had three stories, over 40 rooms, a large bar, and a dining room. Operated for many years by wharfinger Fred Dahnken, the hotel was torn down in 1939 to build a post office, which, for political reasons, never materialized.

RED FRONT SALOON. This saloon was located at 639 Wyatt (Second) Street and owned by Joe Gemur. Despite the temperance concerns of Lester Ludyah Robinson, the last legitimate owner of Los Medanos Rancho, saloons have been in abundance since Antioch's beginning.

SOUTH SIDE OF WYATT STREET, 1910. Palace Drug Company was a fixture in the downtown until the 1970s. The pharmacist mixed the ingredients for prescriptions at the back counter. This was convenient for the patients of Dr. George, whose office can be seen next door. These stores were located in the Heidorn Building. Next to that is the A. Meinken Building constructed in 1905 by the Meinken family. The lower level housed the Vogel Saloon, and the upper rooms were rented out.

FIRST NATIONAL BANK OF ANTIOCH. Located on the southwest corner of Boobar and Wyatt (G and Second) Streets, the bank incorporated in October 1910 and opened for business on January 3, 1911, with J. L. Harding as president. The building also housed the Antioch Bank of Savings, used by merchants. Both banks moved to the southeast corner of Third and G Streets in 1947 and merged with Wells Fargo Bank in 1954.

ANTIOCH CASH STORE. The Belshaw family removed this building on the southeast corner of Boobar and Wyatt (Second and G) Streets in 1905 to allow for construction of the modern, brick Belshaw Building and Theatre on the same site.

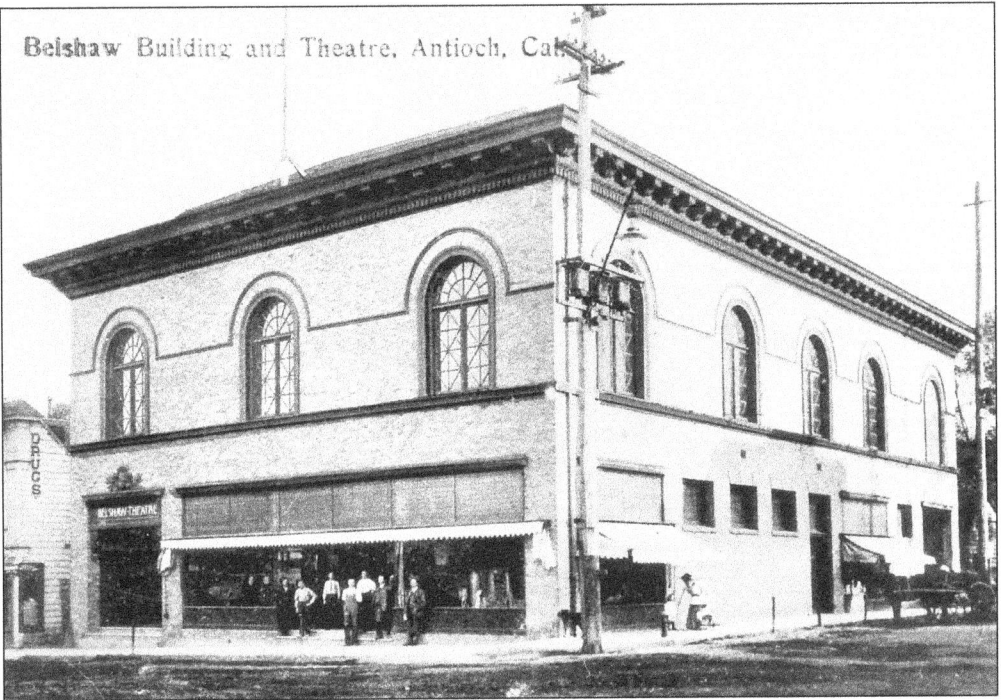

BELSHAW BUILDING. The upstairs theatre was used for high school graduations, dances, and basketball games for many years. This area has served as meeting facilities for Antioch Masonic Lodge No. 175 since their purchase of the building in 1923.

CARMAN AND ISRAEL GROCERIES. Established in the 1870s by Jewish merchants G. S. Carman and Oscar Israel, the building was operated as a general mercantile store. It is the second oldest commercial building remaining in town and later became the Jack Wolfe Hardware Store.

L. MEYER DRY GOODS STORE. Originally Kimball Dry Goods, the store was located on the northwest corner of Boobar and Wyatt (Second and H) Streets. Operated by the Meyer brothers, the business developed a local reputation as the largest and best-equipped general merchandise store in the area. Leopold and Gabriel Meyer sold groceries, clothing, and hardware.

ANTIOCH TELEPHONE EXCHANGE. In 1884, J. Rio Baker installed Antioch's first telephone in his Antioch Drug Store. The Sunset Telephone Company (Antioch Telephone Exchange) was established with six subscribers in 1892. By 1904, Antioch had all-night telephone service, and in 1907 an enlarged switchboard was installed. The first telephone numbers were given to subscribers in 1908.

TELEPHONE EXCHANGE STAFF. The oldest known photograph of the Antioch Telephone Exchange shows three of the five operators in 1912: Alva Biglow Hodgson, Hazel O'Mara, and Mrs. Elam. Their office was reported to be located on Second Street. This second photograph, from the 1940s, shows the office at the corner of G and Fourth Streets, where the telephone operators mural is located today.

JUETT'S ICE CREAM PARLOR. Juett's later became Joe Ross Ice Cream Parlor. Also located on G Street, between Second and Third Streets, was Antioch Notions and Ernie Meyers Department Store.

G Street, Looking North from Fourth. Pictured in the 1950s are an early Ben Franklin, Nash Pharmacy, and Rexall Drugstore. Across Third is a meat market in the Donlon Building.

Brown and Baker Hardware Store. This store later became Antioch Hardware and Furniture, then Trembath and Fredrickson, and, finally, Howse Hardware.

HOWSE HARDWARE. Until it closed in 1987, the building was occupied by Famous Fashions, a popular women's apparel store. The building still stands on the northeast corner of Second and G Streets.

TREMBATH AND FREDERICKSON. This is the interior of the store during one of its many reincarnations, from hardware to general store to clothing store.

ARATA BUILDING/TOWNE HOUSE HOTEL. Constructed in 1905 by Joseph Arata, on the southwest corner of I and Second Streets, this building has been known as the Commercial Hotel, the Antioch Hotel, and, in the 1950s, the Towne House Hotel. An intense fire (believed to have been started by vagrants) destroyed the building in October 1998.

DOMESTIC FRENCH LAUNDRY. The business was taken over by B. Taillefer on May 1, 1925. A 1950 advertisement listed it as the oldest operating laundry in Antioch. Coauthor Charles Bohakel remembers picking up the church linens as an altar boy at Holy Rosary Church in the late 1950s.

EL CAMPANIL THEATRE. The Palace Hotel was leveled in 1926 to allow the construction of the El Campanil Theatre in 1928. The leveling exposed the Chinese tunnels below Second Street. Ferd Stamm and Ralph Beede opened the theater on November 1, 1928. A popular vaudeville theater, many early performers signed their names on the walls of the basement dressing rooms. Names such as Sally Rand, Roy Rogers, Edgar Bergen, Charlie McCarthy, and Al Jolson can still be seen today. The theater is currently being renovated.

TYLER HOTEL/EL DORADO HOTEL. Built out of locally made brick by N. A. Tyler, rooms rented for 25¢ to 50¢ daily, and meals cost 25¢. Referred to by old-timers as the Bucket of Blood Saloon, it reportedly housed a bordello on the upper level.

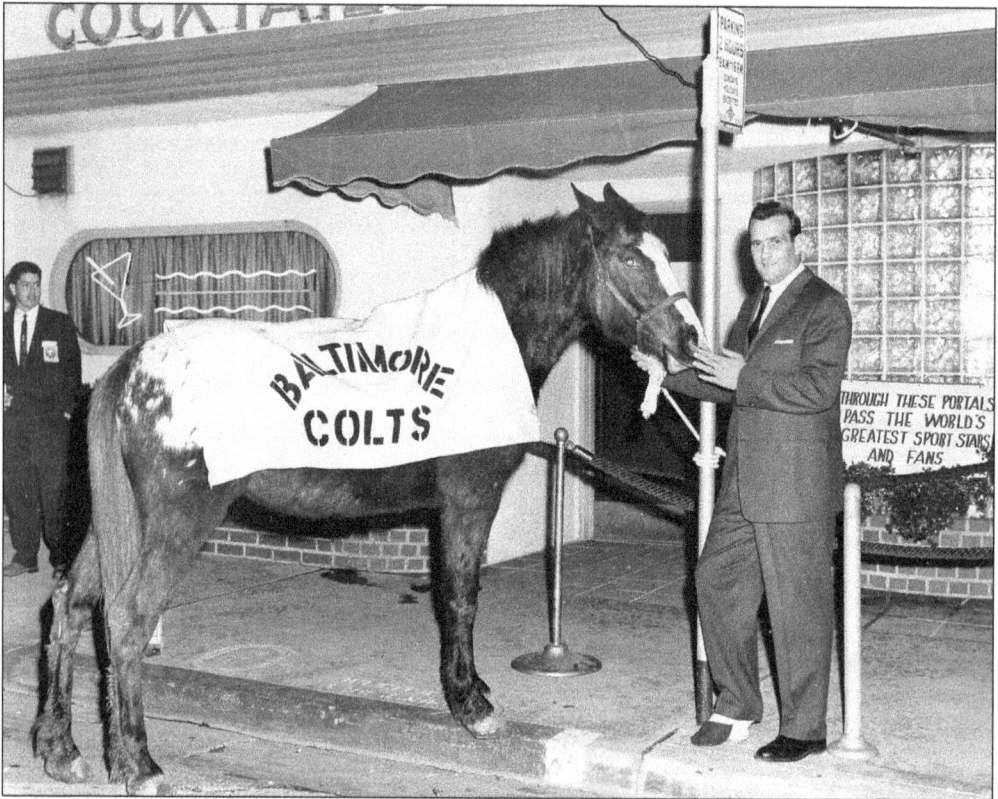

MARCHETTI'S RESTAURANT. Located on I Street, between First and Second Streets, the Marchetti family established their Marchetti Club dining hall in the lower level of the old Tyler Building. It became one of the most popular family-style dining restaurants in Antioch, famous for its seven-course meal. All-American Gino Marchetti, of the Baltimore Colts, was raised in Antioch. The building was removed in 1987 and replaced with the present PG&E office buildings.

ANTIOCH PROFESSIONAL AND BUSINESSMEN. Pictured around 1946, from left to right, are (first row) Harold Turner, Howard Lauritzen, and Larry Mehaffey; (second row) Joe Viera, Charlie Hornback, Tom Milan, and Vic Parachini; (third row) Jim Taylor, Joe Cesa, and Mike Grief; (fourth row) Leo O'Hara, Earl Stevens, Carl McElhaney, unidentified, and Dr. Nevius.

CORNER GROCERIES. Before supermarkets, the corner grocery was depended upon for everything from milk and staples for Mom to penny candy and school lunches for the kids. Clark's Grocery (originally Todd's Grocery) was located on the southwest corner of Nineteenth and D Streets.

STANDARD OIL GAS STATION. A young Bob Swain owned and operated Antioch's first bona fide service station built for the exclusive purpose of selling gasoline, on the northeast corner of Fifth and G Streets.

PACINI SALES AND SERVICE. This business was located on the northeast corner of Seventh and A Streets. Note the City of Antioch water tower, left, in this photograph.

BESWICK INSURANCE. Bob Beswick stands in front of his first insurance office on the southeast corner of Fourth and G Streets. This *c.* 1950 image was the source for the mural across the street depicting telephone operators. In the mural, Beswick seems to serve as the unofficial greeter of downtown.

RAHLFS MOTOR COMPANY. Located on the southeast corner of Wilbur Avenue and A Street, the Rahlfs Motor Company was heralded as one of the most modern and beautiful buildings in the area in 1948. Originally a showroom for the Hudson dealership with an auto repair shop, the building is virtually unrecognizable today.

FERRANTE FAMILY. Alfredo Ferranti purchased 10 acres from the Meinken family on the southwest corner of Eighteenth and A Streets. His children, the Enea-Ferranti-Cerri families, subsequently operated the Enea Dairy distribution business on this site until it was sold to build one of the earliest shopping centers in Antioch.

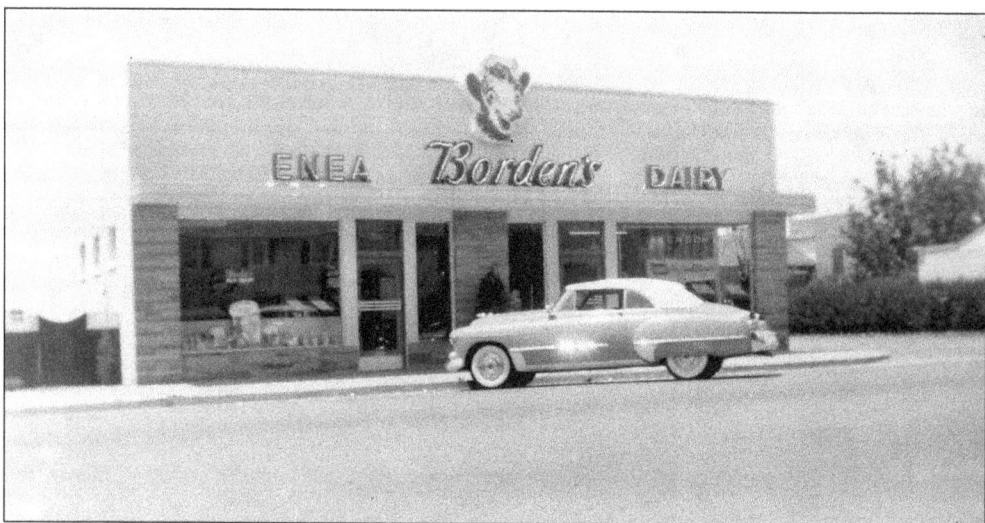

ENEA BORDEN DAIRY. In the late 1950s, the Enea Borden Dairy distribution operation moved to the downtown area, where it is still owned and operated by the Enea family, now as the Crystal Cream and Butter Company, at Sixth and O Streets.

ANTIOCH SQUARE SHOPPING STRIP MALL. In March 1964, business leaders displayed designs for the new Antioch Square Center to be located at the northeast corner of Eighteenth and A Streets. Pictured, from left to right, are Jim Davi, unidentified, Bob Carkeek, Dorothy Shelton, Bill Bassett, unidentified, and Ollie Hamlin. The earlier construction of the Eastwood Mall (Lucky Shopping Center) on the southwest corner of Eighteenth and A, along with the Antioch Square Shopping Center, signaled the demise of the robust downtown commercial area.

Seven

INDUSTRY

The first industrial developments centered around the manufacture of brick and related clay products using the area's ample supply of sand and clay. Sand was abundant in the Mount Diablo foothills and along the waterfront near the now Wilbur Avenue. Hard and soft clays of various colors were also available. After the 1906 earthquake, Antioch became a major supplier of the sewer pipes, stove pipes, clay tiles, and bricks needed to rebuild San Francisco.

With the abundance of grain growing in the area, a few early industrial ventures were devoted to taking care of the thirst of the townspeople. In 1869, the Antioch Distillery Company was started by George Russell, William Knight, and George Gruenwald. In 1870, Mr. Jost purchased the distillery that was located on C Street, between Third and Fourth Streets, including a pier to the east that extended out into the river. By 1879, its production reached 3,000 gallons of whiskey per day.

Paper manufacturing from straw came to Antioch in 1889, when M. D. Keeney and Sons established the Enterprise Paper Mill along the San Joaquin River in the western part of town, between L and O Streets. The plant became operational in 1890, producing about five tons of straw paper per day when purchased in 1902 by Peter Brown and Sons.

In 1912, the Paraffin Paint Company of San Francisco purchased the mill and incorporated as the California Paper and Board Mill. In 1929, the Paraffin Companies and the National Paper Products Company combined to form Fibreboard Products, Inc. In the 1950s, the community had a population of 12,500, and 6,500 people worked for Fibreboard plants and subsidiaries in Antioch.

The company also purchased Riverview Union High School building in 1947, and it became known as Fibreboard Research Division. During the war years, wax-coated cardboard later led to the development of the milk carton.

In the late 1950s, other related companies would construct plants on Wilbur Avenue, which became known as Industrial Row. The Crown Zellerbach plant, adjacent to the Fibreboard San Joaquin Plant, was built in 1956 and was the largest plant in the world operating exclusively on recycled paper.

Pacific Gas and Electric Company broke ground on Wilbur Avenue for its $51.5 million power plant in 1949. Also in 1956, Kaiser Cement and Gypsum located its wallboard plant on Wilbur Avenue and shipped in raw gypsum ore from the Gulf of California. Neighboring homes became coated with the white powder produced from the smoke stacks and people began to voice environmental concerns.

Smaller service industries that provided a variety of products for the bigger industries began to locate in Antioch in the 1970s. As Antioch became the fastest-growing bedroom community in the county, the heyday of manufacturing, along with the tradition of sons following their fathers into good jobs at local industries, began to give way to an era of suburban sprawl. The population had climbed to over 37,000.

In the first half of the 20th century, the paper industry was the most powerful industry in town, encouraging employees to run for city councils to protect the industry's interests and to always keep the city from annexing the plants into the city limits. Staying outside the city limits kept them free of city fees and taxes. However, due to salt water intrusion from San Francisco Bay into the San Joaquin River, the industries found they needed to purchase clean water from the city. This development, in addition to new environmental protection laws, saw the plants sold and resold and eventually closed. The San Joaquin pulp plant was shut down and dismantled, giving a totally different smell to the community and the surrounding housing. During this period, Fibreboard Products, Inc. purchased Crown Zellerbach, becoming Louisiana Pacific, then Gaylord, and finally Temple-Inland Paper. Glass Containers was sold to Anchor Glass, sold again and closed. Kaiser Gypsum was sold to Domtar and then to Georgia Pacific. Environmental protection and air quality laws required them to install serious filters on all production lines. DuPont closed and dismantled their plant, moving most production to Mississippi.

In 1972, when the Fibreboard plant on L Street closed, 429 employees lost their jobs. By 2004, only 84 paper workers remained employed in town located at the Temple-Inland corrugating plant on Fourth Street. So ended Antioch's industrial age, as the town's main industry became residential building and the population exceeded 100,000.

—Compiled by Charles Bohakel and Elizabeth Rimbault

CALIFORNIA BRICK WORKS. Antioch's first industry was started in 1852 by Job C. McMaster and Mr. Barber. These first brick kilns were built at Wyatt and Robinson (Second and K) Streets and were purchased in 1868 by I. Nicholson, who renamed the company Albion Pottery.

BRICK WORKS KILNS. Other kilns besides those at the California Brick Works were built around town, including Lobree Pottery Works by Isac Lobree, on the north side of Wyatt (Second) Street, between Emerson and Kimball (E and F) Streets; California Pottery, located south of Fulton Shipyards on land owned by the Biglow family; and, by 1890, the Dittell Company, near H Street and the Southern Pacific Railroad. The industry produced red clay bricks, sandstone bricks, chimney and sewer pipes, terra cotta, and stove linings.

JOST DISTILLERY. Workers stand behind finished barrels ready for shipping, and a wagon driver delivers grain for mash. The Jost Distillery was started in the 1800s by Christian Jost (1843–1896), a native of Germany. The 1865 U.S. government survey that established the boundary between Los Meganos Rancho (Marsh) and Los Medanos Rancho (Robinson) shows the Jost Distillery Wharf as the boundary line.

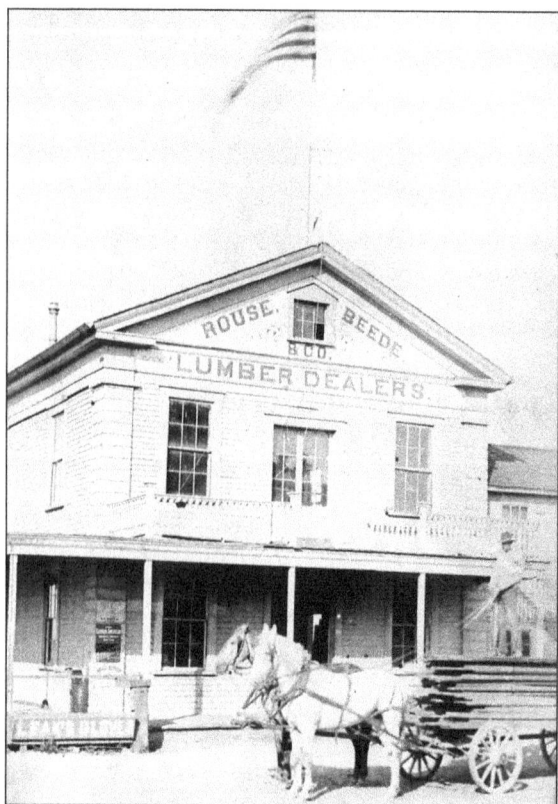

ROUSE AND BEEDE LUMBER. The company was founded in 1864 by the partnership of Galloway and Boobar. In 1877, John Rouse bought the company and named it Rouse, Forman, and Beede Lumber Company. The name was changed to Rouse, Beede, and Abbott Lumber Company about 1880.

ANTIOCH LUMBER COMPANY. The former Antioch Grange building, located at the northeast corner of Wyatt and Emerson (Second and E) Streets, was purchased in 1883. The lumber company has been at this location ever since, making it the oldest business still in operation in Antioch. 1907 saw the incorporation of the Antioch Lumber Company. This is said to be the oldest lumber company in California still doing business in its original location.

HENRY FULLER BEEDE. Mr. Beede was owner of Antioch Lumber Company and former mayor of Antioch.

PLANING MILL. The Antioch Lumber Company added a planing mill about 1904 with the purchase of the former Antioch Distillery building on Third Street, between B and C Streets. The building was destroyed by fire in the 1950s.

CANNERIES. Local canneries included Hickmott Canners in East Antioch, owned by the Russell family; the Davi family's Western Canners on the west side of town, which later became Tillie Lewis, owned by National Can; and the asparagus packing shed on the waterfront between the two canneries adjacent to the Santa Fe Railroad tracks. The pilings of the packing shed can still be seen.

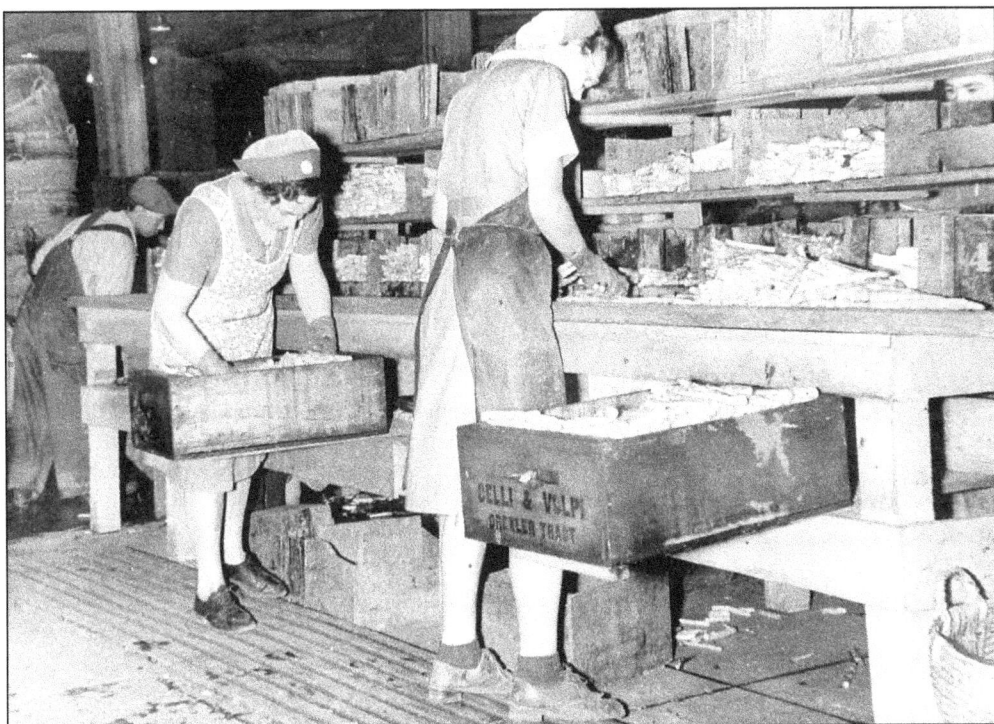

LOCAL LABELS. The large variety of produce grown by local farms provided Hickmott Canning Company and its workers with continuous work from spring through fall. Here women pack spring asparagus for shipping.

SNOW WHITE
PEELED

SIGNATURE BRAND

CANNERY LADY. Dedicated in 1996, this monument by Elizabeth MacQueen honors the many women who withstood the heat and long hours of the summers as they processed the fruits of the delta. According to the Smithsonian Institution, the *Cannery Lady* became the first non-military commemorative to a working woman in the western region of the United States. The sale of terra cotta tiles listing the names of former workers and community members financed the commission and completion of the statue, making it the first privately funded art project in the city of Antioch. The inscribed tiles form a plaza surrounding the base of the statue. Stars on the tiles indicate names of cannery workers.

GLASS CONTAINERS, 1947. Glass Containers, Inc., a division of Fibreboard Products, was constructed in the winter of 1947 on the north side Fourth Street at O Street to help meet new consumer demands after the war. Note the Riverview Union High School building (current Antioch Historical Society Museum) to the west of this construction.

GLASS CONTAINERS. In the summer of 1948, the first bottle rolled off the assembly line at Glass Containers, Inc. It was a 10-ounce Dennison chili sauce bottle.

FULTON SHIPYARD. Originally owned by the Jarvis Brothers, the shipyard was located in the area of Harkinson's Point in the late 1800s. The business was sold to Christian August Lauritzen Sr. in 1918 and then resold to Les Fulton and became the Fulton Shipyards in 1924. Following his death in 1951, his wife, Angeline Fulton, became the only woman shipbuilder in the United States.

ATLAS ENGINE. Christian Lauritzen is pictured with one cylinder of the five-ton Atlas diesel engine being shipped to the Smithsonian Institution, Washington, D.C., in April 1959.

ENTERPRISE PAPER MILL. Founded in 1889 by M.D. Keeney and Sons and operational in 1890, this plant was located on L Street, between the Santa Fe Railroad and Fourth Street.

PULP MILL IN ACTION. Purchased in 1902 by Peter Brown and Sons, the Enterprise Paper Mill made pulp, with the end product of cardboard, from straw.

ANTIOCH'S FIRST BASEBALL TEAM, 1890S. Pictured here are, from left to right, (first row) Jerry Donlon, Elmer Page; (second row) Jay Belshaw, Frank Wills, Gave Meyer, and Charles Sweeney (later city marshal); (third row) Sen. C. M. Belshaw, Dave Wall, Joseph Ross, Pete Grennan, and unidentified.

FIBREBOARD PLANT. The plant was built adjacent to the Santa Fe Railroad and east of the Riverview Union High School. In the 1920s, bales of straw were stacked well away from the buildings but near the water tower, in case of fire. The plant operated until 1972, when the majority of workers were moved to the Stockton plant. The site is now home to the Antioch Police Department.

FIBREBOARD PRODUCTS, SAN JOAQUIN PLANT. Fibreboard constructed a second plant on Wilbur Avenue in 1947. The company had switched from straw to wood-chip pulp production, and this plant, which included its own power plant, eventually became the largest kraft pulp and paperboard plant in California. At one time, it was the only pulp mill south of Oregon. Its pungent odor became the source of constant complaints and environmental concerns by local citizens.

PRODUCT RESEARCH AT FIBREBOARD. During the war years, research was conducted at Fibreboard Research in Antioch (current location of the Antioch Historical Society Museum) on how to produce alternative packaging for cold beverages and ice cream. They patented a method of applying wax coatings to cardboard containers that spawned the first milk, juice, and ice cream containers. Prior to 1950, all liquid containers were glass or tin. Antioch is the "home of the milk carton."

FIBREBOARD RESEARCHERS, 1947. Pictured on the steps of the former school are, from left to right, (first row) unidentified janitor, Edward C. Jennings Jr., Dr. Howard Bruce, Dr. Kenneth, and Orville ?; (second row) Bill Woods, David Edwards, secretary ?, E. P. Cox, and unidentified.

FIBREBOARD RESEARCH.
Analytical research chemist
Edward C. Jennings Jr. is pictured
here *c.* 1951 in the Fibreboard
research laboratory, now the lower
floor of the Antioch Historical
Society Museum.

ANTIOCH BASEBALL TEAM, 1921. If a man was on the baseball team, he was guaranteed a job at Fibreboard. If he was an especially good player, he worked in the preferred jobs. The paper company often determined the community's well being, with jobs, recreational activities like baseball, and politics. Many of its employees were elected to the city council.

Eight

RIVER LIFE AND TRANSPORTATION

The river prevented the early town of Antioch from dying. With no roads or surrounding populated areas, Antioch's earliest settlers were completely dependent upon the river for food, supplies, news, settlers, and industries to sustain the town with employment. Shortly after its settlement, a small dock was built along the waterfront that allowed the town to eventually become a shipper and a receiver of the growing river commerce.

J. W. Galloway built a wharf at the foot of E Street in 1859. In 1871, the Antioch Grange also built a wharf at the foot of D Street. Both wharves were later connected and used by the Antioch Lumber Company to accommodate lumber schooners from Northern California and the Pacific Northwest.

Coal was first discovered in 1859 by William C. Israel at Horse Haven, about 6 miles south of Antioch. After the discovery of additional fields in the hills to the south and southeast of Antioch, the Empire Coal Mine and Railroad Company built its coal wharf at the foot of F Street to load barges for shipment to San Francisco, Sacramento, and Stockton. The coal from the Mount Diablo Coal fields, the largest in the state, made possible the early industrial development of the San Francisco Bay Area.

From the 1860s to the 1880s, wheat was king in Contra Costa County. Transported to Port Costa from Antioch by river steamer and train, the golden grains filled the holds of windjammers from the United Kingdom and Western Europe. This encouraged the building of a number of wharves along the Antioch waterfront as storage. The Santa Fe Railroad built a wharf, grain warehouse, and packing sheds between G and H Streets, where asparagus and other produce were packed. The Antioch Wharf (City Wharf), between H and I Streets, was used by most passenger and freight vessels that stopped at Antioch. The Riverview Restaurant occupies it today. East of Antioch, along Wilbur Avenue, a number of docks and piers were built and equipped with conveyor belts to facilitate the loading of sand for shipment throughout the Bay Area. This sand was considered among the finest in the world for making macadam roadbeds.

The Central Pacific Railroad (later the Southern Pacific and now the Union Pacific) had a branch line (San Pablo and Tulare Railroad) that arrived in Antioch in 1878. Santa Fe Railroad (its branch line was known as the San Francisco and San Joaquin Valley Railroad) selected Antioch as its eastern terminus in 1900. The tracks are still busy with freights and Amtrak San Joaquin passenger trains. With the closing down of Greyhound and Gibson bus service years ago, the train is now the only connection to the valley communities and southern California other than the highway.

The Antioch waterfront witnessed the West's greatest era of steamboating with paddle wheelers, like the Delta Queen and Delta King, bound for the ports of Stockton and Sacramento. Later shallow-draft stern wheelers were used by the River Lines to transport freight and passengers to Antioch and other river communities on a daily basis.

The Jarvis brothers built a shipyard along the Antioch waterfront east of Harkinson's Point (Smith's Point/Rogers' Point) in the town's early years. Christian August Lauritzen Sr. bought the shipyard in 1918. Frank Leslie Fulton purchased the complex in 1924 and built his home at the location. During World War II, Fulton Shipyard was awarded contracts from the navy to build 13 wooden coastal minesweepers. When Frank Leslie (Les) Fulton died in 1952, management of the shipyards was taken over by his wife, Angeline, and their son Leslie Fulton. The 1960s would see Fulton Shipyard involved in a new type of transportation—construction of giant cranes that were used to build and launch rockets into space at Cape Canaveral (Cape Kennedy), Florida.

Prior to the construction of a bridge, Captain Christian A. Lauritzen Sr. used his vessel *Sherman* to provide a "highway" link between Antioch and Sherman Island in Sacramento County. The *Sherman* had a capacity of 10 automobiles and made a trip every two hours.

The Antioch Bridge (Antioch–Sherman Island Toll Bridge) opened on January 1, 1926, as the first toll bridge in California. It united central and northern California, linked Antioch to the delta, and was the first overwater crossing connecting the north and south sides of the San Joaquin River.

—Compiled by Charles Bohakel

SAILING SHIPS, 1870S. The barks *B. P. Cheney* (1874), *Pactolus* (1891), *St. Kathrine* (1890), and *Hecla* (1877) were moored across the San Joaquin River from Antioch, near Kimball Island. When vandalism caused them to be viewed as hazardous and attractive nuisances, they were burned in place and sunk. This photograph was probably taken in the 1930s.

EMPIRE COAL MINE ROUNDHOUSE. Connecting the coal-mining communities of Judsonville, West Hartley, and Stewartville, some six miles south, to the Antioch waterfront was the narrow-gauge (36 inches between rails) Empire Mine Railroad. The roundhouse and blacksmith shop were located on the southwest corner of F and Fourth Streets.

ORIGINAL CREW OF THE EMPIRE RAILROAD. Pictured in 1878 are, from left to right, Bill Bullock, fireman; Elmer Page, brakeman; S. H. McKellips, engineer; and Putnam Reed, brakeman.

EMPIRE COAL MINE RAILROAD COAL WHARF. On January 6, 1878, the first load of 400 tons of coal was delivered by the railroad to Antioch's coal wharf. By mid-1888, between 2,000 to 2,500 tons of coal arrived at the wharf for shipping each month. The railroad stopped running in 1897, and the mines closed around 1902.

ANTIOCH LUMBER COMPANY WHARF. To the east in this *c.* 1905 photograph is the Jost Distillery Wharf and in the distance, Harkinson's Point (also called Smith's Point or Rogers' Point).

ANTIOCH LUMBER COMPANY. The view to the west shows the Antioch Lumber Company as a full-throttle business.

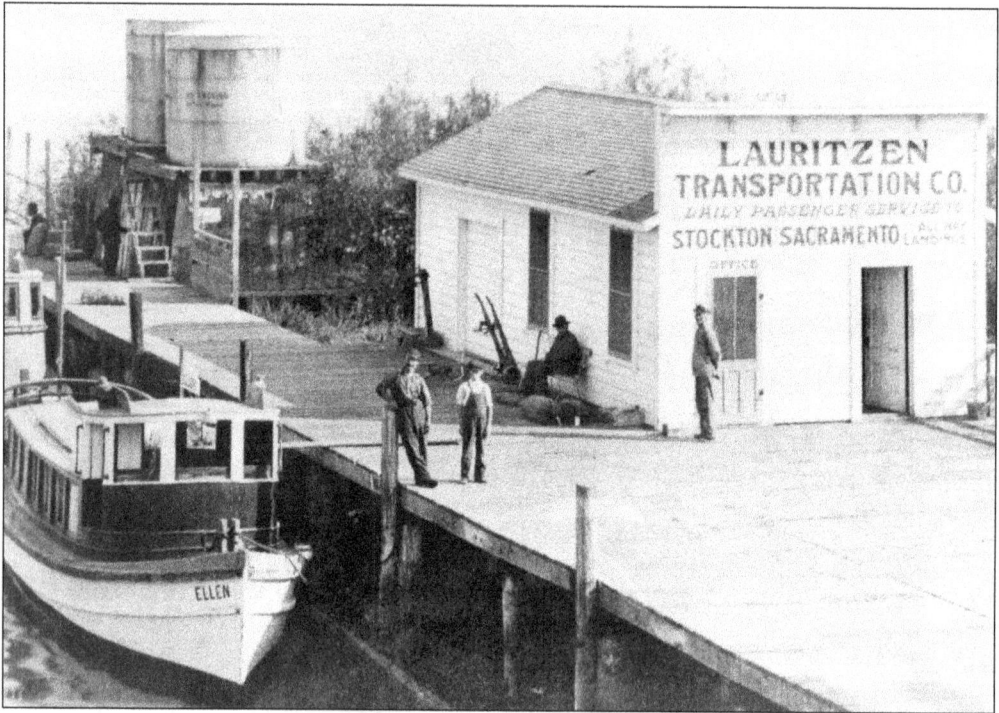

LAURITZEN TRANSPORTATION COMPANY. Developed by the city, the municipal wharf at the foot of J Street was used by the Lauritzen Transportation Company, a pioneer in river passenger travel.

SOUTHERN PACIFIC DEPOT. The late 1960s would see the station removed and commercial development put in its place. By the end of the 21st century, idle cars would sit on the tracks to maintain railroad easements in the hopes that the rail alignment would become part of the Bay Area Rapid Transit system for commuters to the Bay Area. This photograph was taken around 1905.

Santa Fe Depot of Antioch, Early 1900s. Built by Santa Fe on Front Street at Parsons (First Street at J about 1902, the depot is shown from the riverside, or track side), as the community anxiously awaits the arriving train. This picture may have been taken at the dedication of the depot. The metal tank was built to hold raw river water for the steam locomotives. The station was destroyed by fire in 1979. The lower photograph shows the Hard House across the street.

JARVIS BROTHERS SHIPYARD, LATER FULTON SHIPYARD. Numerous barges, wooden tugs, fishing boats and river freighters were built there, including the first diesel-powered boat to operate on the San Joaquin and Sacramento Rivers. This was the only shipyard between San Francisco and Sacramento equipped to do maintenance and repair work on wooden vessels.

HICKMOTT CANNERY, 1920S. Canneries lined the waterfront and dumped debris directly into the river. Catfish were healthy and abundant in the waters adjacent to the canneries.

FULTON SHIPYARD. The yard is pictured before the war contracts, tug boats, dredgers, and barges. In the far background, a faint Antioch Bridge is visible, dating this photograph to after 1926.

Lauritzen Bros. Launch Empress & Dredger Alameda, Antioch, Cal.

LAUNCH. This postcard shows the Lauritzen Brothers's launch of the *Empress* and the dredger *Alameda*. The 70-foot *Empress* was built in 1912 and was the pride of the fleet of Lauritzen Transportation Company.

ANTIOCH BRIDGE UNDER CONSTRUCTION. Taken in 1925 from the bridge of the *Belvedere* by Harry Carton, first mate of the *Belvedere*, this rare photograph shows the construction of the first Antioch Bridge. The bridge opened the delta to truck and automobile traffic for the first time and was known as "The Golden Link."

CALIFORNIA LIMITED: THE SAN PABLO ON THE SAN JOAQUIN RIVER. Ferryboats were a mainstay of travel from the cities on San Francisco Bay. The long run upriver encouraged riverboat captains to test their skills in competition. During the heyday of racing, lives of both crew and passengers were lost when ship engines exploded with the request for "more steam!" as they raced up the river.

EL PRIMERO AT ANTIOCH LUMBER COMPANY WHARF, 1897. Launched in San Francisco Bay in 1893 and owned by Edward W. Hopkins, nephew of Mark Hopkins of the Big Four, El Primero winter-quartered at the Antioch Lumber Company Wharf from 1895 to 1906.

MARSH LANDING. A post office at Marsh Landing operated from September 1852 to 1854. It was on the river, approximately three miles east of present-day Antioch. The wharf was built to supply John Marsh's ranch.

MINESWEEPER NO. 448. This ship was launched at Fulton Shipyard, 1953.

ANGELINE FULTON. After her husband, Frank Leslie Fulton, died in 1951, Mrs. Fulton became the only female shipbuilder in the United States. In addition to a contract for minesweepers, other contracts resulted in 27 vessels being built for the navy and earning the shipyard the navy's "E" award for excellence six consecutive times. After the war, the work switched to the repair and reconversion of ships for the navy, army, and war shipping administration.

VOCATIONAL TRAINING. Students of Antioch High School in the 1950s learned the trade of shipbuilding in a program adjacent to Rogers' Point, west of Fulton Shipyard. Les Fulton supplied the lumber and engine for the project, then bought back the finished boat each year. Good students were guaranteed work as shipwrights at the shipyard following graduation.

RECREATION ON THE RIVER. While beaches provided sand that was shipped for use in paving or glass manufacturing, they also provided a place for picnicking or sunbathing. Antioch Beach, located east of Fulton Shipyard off Wilbur Avenue, was a popular summer spot for Antioch residents. Huts were constructed on the pier as changing rooms for swimmers. Residents built summer cabins and spent many hot days at the rivers edge. Now remaining beaches are closed to the public for the protection of the Antioch Dunes Evening Primrose and Lange's Metalmark Butterfly, both endangered species.

FORMER ABUNDANCE, 1950s. The delta marshes and waterways, part of the Pacific Flyway, still draw all manner of waterfowl for hunters and photographers.

ICE SKATING ON THE SAN JOAQUIN. William H. Graham tests out the ice at Big Break, east of Antioch, in December 1936, when the river's edge froze over.

CRANES FOR CAPE CANAVERAL. The 1960s brought a change from shipbuilding to giant crane building for Fulton Shipyards. The huge cranes were used at Cape Canaveral (Cape Kennedy) for the construction and launching of rocket ships.

SOUTHERN PACIFIC RAILROAD FERRY SOLANO. Built in 1879 and once the largest train ferry in the world, the *Solano* carried freight and passenger trains across the Carquinez Straits between Port Costa and Benicia. In 1932, due to the construction of the Southern Pacific railroad bridge, the *Solano* was towed to Antioch. Joe Cesa later created a breakwater for his Antioch Boat Harbor (Tommy's Harbor), on the west side of Harkinson's Point (Smith's/Rogers' Point) by sinking the ship at the opening.

ROGERS' POINT IN ITS PRIME. John Rogers raised the house to a second story, built the sea wall, walkway, and detached garage, all before the sinking of the *Solano* just west of the home at the mouth of Tommy's Harbor.

WATERFRONT, C. 1950. Pilings are all that are left from an earlier pier located between F and G Streets. Fire in the early 1950s destroyed the Antioch Hotel, which had been located at the corner of G and First Streets.

H STREET ALONG THE SANTA FE TRACKS, C. 1950. The Riverview Restaurant was its own island prior to the building of a rear deck for parking. There is a parking area between the restaurant and the river that is actually the City Wharf. Between I Street and L Streets were scows. Western Canners and a small marina were on the west side of L Street. The point later became the site of Humphrey's Restaurant and the City of Antioch Marina. The tracks to the left with spurs for the packing shed, the Santa Fe water tank, depot, and Fibreboard smokestacks show that downtown was still a busy hub of industry in the 1950s.

WAR MEMORIAL. Built to mark the Victory Highway and to commemorate servicemen and women lost during World War I, this memorial was dedicated on May 31, 1926, at the intersection of Bridgehead Road and State Highway 4. Due to road improvements, the memorial was moved to the fairgrounds in Antioch in the 1970s. Another marker of the Victory Highway is the rock wall built around the city park at Tenth and A Streets.

URIL "COMPY" COMPOMIZZO, ACTIVIST. Known for his work with organizing fishing derbies and his advocacy for clean water for the San Joaquin River, Compy sits in front of the fishing pier named for him. He was founder of the youth program "Get Hooked on Fishing, Not on Drugs." (Photograph by Jose Carlos Fajardo, *Contra Costa Times.*)

UNTITLED, **(1861–1962).** Warren Rollins painted this view of Roger's Point in Antioch in 1881. Born in Carson City, Nevada, Rollins was raised in Antioch. He was known mainly for his paintings of Native Americans and scenes of the Southwest. He became known as the "Dean of Taos and Santa Fe Art Colonies." The painting was not seen outside of Antioch until the late 1990s, when the Dean Lesher Foundation provided a grant for its restoration by the DeYoung Museum in San Francisco.

ANTIOCH DUNES EVENING PRIMROSE. The Antioch Dunes National Wildlife Refuge is located on the southern shore of the San Joaquin River, east of Antioch. Covering about one-fourth of their original area, access to the dunes is restricted for the protection of endangered species. The Antioch Dunes Evening Primrose, the Contra Costa Wallflower, and the Lange's Metalmark Butterfly are found in this area alone.

Nine

THE NEW CENTURY

In the new century, the needs of Antioch's residents are being met by the increased goods and services provided by several new shopping areas. The newest, Slatten Ranch, coordinated the meeting of three communities at the intersection of Lone Tree Way and Empire Avenue, just down the road from the Highway 4 Bypass.

Residential growth has spread further east and south, and newer residents have come to the area to find a small-town atmosphere with reasonably affordable housing for the San Francisco Bay Area. Ironically, each new home replaces what was once farmland, increases home values, and decreases the community's ability to maintain its small-town atmosphere. Developers and city officials have worked throughout the last decade to answer the challenges of producing balance, requiring open space, trails, and parks as part of all new developments.

By it all, the river continues to flow. Once teeming with commercial fishermen and sailing ships that filled their holds at Antioch wharves, the river now serves as a commerce highway for freighters carrying goods to Stockton and Sacramento. The future may see the river become a transportation highway with ferries providing commuter services. Even train tracks, once used for shipping products to market, are being reconsidered as answers to transportation questions.

The need to educate Antioch's children has been a primary concern since the days of the founding fathers. The number of schools has increased tenfold, and more are in the planning stages. Doctors, dentists, specialists, and all types of professionals abound in the community, providing the services needed by a growing population. Along our southern city limits new and improved golf courses have been created and assist in maintaining open space. Of course, rattlesnakes and pumas are not unusual sightings as residential growth invades their territory in the shadow of Mount Diablo. But gone are the grizzly bear and the Miwok people, the mining industry and the coal trains, the paper industry and the pulp mill, the shipping wharves and the river-polluting canneries, Chinatown's river shanties and the blighted waterfront.

Today's residents are encouraged to rediscover the river and historic downtown, to partake of the recreational pleasures of the Delta and maintain that small-town feeling within the neighborhoods, to put down roots and enjoy being a part of this community that so enjoys the stories of newer residents coming from around the world. Residents and government officials alike strive to maintain a fine balance between personal rights, property rights, the environment, the need for jobs, businesses, and improved transportation.

The job of the historian is to show the past in the hopes of improving the future. It is the goal and the mission of the Antioch Historical Society to maintain that history for future generations at the site of the Antioch Historical Museum, once Riverview Union High School. The dream of the Smith brothers is as alive today as it was 154 years ago, and the history of the City of Antioch is still in the making. (Compiled by Elizabeth Rimbault.)

THE RODDY RANCH GOLF CLUB. This development is Antioch's greatest political question of the new century. Long in the sphere of influence of the City of Antioch, the golf course was developed while still technically in the county area. City and county politicians have battled over the area's annexation (including the subsequent upscale housing built around the golf course) to the City of Antioch, while newer residents have pushed to hold the Urban Limit Line, which has already been adjusted to exclude Roddy Ranch.

LAST PAPER WORKER. Rather symbolically, the last paper worker, Rubin Alvernaz, appears engulfed by machinery as he finishes a shift and one of the last shipments of cardboard to be made in Antioch. The last mill closed under the ownership of Temple-Inland Paper on May 7, 2005, eliminating the jobs of the last 84 paper workers in the community. This ended 116 years of papermaking in Antioch, with an all-time high workforce of 6,500 in the 1960s.

www.ingramcontent.com/pod-product-compliance
Lightning Source LLC
Chambersburg PA
CBHW080549110426
42813CB00006B/1254